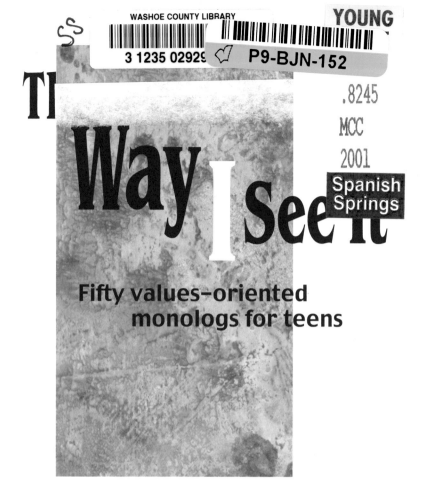

The Way I See It

Fifty values-oriented monologs for teens

Kimberly A. McCormick

MERIWETHER PUBLISHING LTD.
Colorado Springs, Colorado

Meriwether Publishing Ltd., Publisher
P.O. Box 7710
Colorado Springs, CO 80933-7710

Editor: Theodore O. Zapel
Typesetting: Sue Trinko
Cover design: Janice Melvin

© Copyright MMI Meriwether Publishing Ltd.
Printed in the United States of America
First Edition

Library of Congress Cataloging-in-Publication Data

McCormick, Kimberly A. (Kimberly Ann), 1960-
    The way I see it : 50 values-oriented monologs for teens / Kimberly A. McCormick.
    p. cm.
    ISBN 1-56608-072-X (pbk.)
    1. Conduct of life--Study and teaching--Juvenile literature. 2. Teenagers--Conduct of life--Juvenile literature. [1. Conduct of life.] I. Title.

BF637.C5 M358 2001
170'.835--dc21

                                  2001030361

1   2   3   4   5   01   02   03   04

This collection of monologs is dedicated to my teenage daughter, Kaycee. I admire her strong opinions on all issues, many of which I've used in order to create such realistic monologs.

Contents

Introduction

The Way I See It provides students with monologs to be used in drama classrooms, language arts classrooms or wherever the environment lends itself to discussing today's issues. Reading, writing, listening and speaking are all parts of the learning method that *The Way I See It* provides.

Students are asked to deliver a monolog which presents an opinion about a teen issue of today. All of the monologs may be performed in the classroom without props. After the presentation, class members are asked questions related to the topic of the monolog. Questions follow each monolog. The teacher may choose to facilitate a classroom discussion on the topic. Students can offer their opinions regarding the problems presented.

It is my hope that from these discussions students may come to understand that it is necessary to view problems from the perspective of all those involved. Also, there may be more than one way to solve a problem. It's important to listen to others' points of view, and to show respect when others' opinions differ from your own.

I hope you enjoy incorporating the art of theatre into your classroom as much as my students and I do.

Kimberly McCormick

A Promise to Non-Violence

1   What's happening to our world? What's wrong with
2 some of the kids in our schools? It's hard to believe that
3 kids my age are bringing guns to school and killing each
4 other. Every time I turn on the television and hear about
5 another school shooting, I get filled with all these feelings.
6 I can't even put how I feel into words. It's like I'm angry
7 and sad at the same time.

8   On one hand I'm so mad at the gunmen, because it's
9 hard for me to understand how anyone could kill
10 somebody. But on the other hand, it's so sad to think that
11 these kids are so unhappy and confused that they feel they
12 have to resort to violence.

13   We all get upset and depressed at times. Let's face it,
14 life's not always easy or fair. At the risk of sounding like
15 my parents, I have to say that I think movies, music, video
16 games, you know, all those things, have something to do
17 with this. If you disagree, just ask yourself this question:
18 When you're sad about something and you listen to a sad
19 song, don't you get even more depressed? And if you want
20 to get in a better mood, isn't there a favorite song that
21 always lifts your spirits when you hear it? Don't you think
22 kids who are angry, and then watch some crazy movie with
23 fighting and killing, will only become more upset?

24   And what about the Internet? You can learn how to do
25 almost anything. There really needs to be some kind of
26 control over it. I know, I know, that would take away an
27 American's freedom of speech and press. Well, to tell you
28 the truth, I think some people should have those freedoms
29 taken away. Why can't you lose that freedom if you abuse
30 it?

1   Something needs to be done. I really don't want to
2   feel as if I'm coming to jail every morning when I enter
3   the school. What is all this? Armed guards in the school?
4   Metal detectors? Drug raids and locker searches? No
5   wonder more and more parents are choosing to home
6   school their children. Heck, if things keep getting worse,
7   I don't even think I'll have any children.
8   I really am starting to sound like an adult, aren't I?
9   I guess that means I need to stop talking, but think
10   about some of the things I said, OK? I guess I'm just
11   wondering what kids like you and me can do to help. I
12   don't want to go to school scared. Do you?

What's Your Opinion?

Share what your school system does to make you feel safe there.

How do you feel about the influences of the Internet, movies, video games, etc., upon school violence? Do you believe human rights would be violated if restrictions were to be placed upon these things? Explain.

Are you willing to join the nationwide campaign to promise not to participate in any school violence? Would you be willing to promise to report any warning signs you may witness regarding violence in your school? If so, please write such a statement.

Cheating

1   Right now my stomach is sick. I just left the awards
2 assembly at my high school. You'd think I'd be happy. I
3 won the school's Citizenship Award and top honors for my
4 grades. I earned ten thousand dollars in scholarship money
5 for college. My whole family was there cheering for me. I
6 felt really good about myself until this kid in my class
7 named John started receiving all of his awards.
8   You see, John is what I'd call your stereotypical jock.
9 He's built gorgeous, he's really cute and is the star of our
10 football, basketball and track teams. He's sort of every
11 girl's dream.
12   During football season John started talking to me
13 before and after history class. I was surprised, but I loved
14 the attention. I was even stupid enough to start fantasizing
15 that maybe John cared about me as more than just a
16 friend. That was a mistake.
17   All John wanted me for was my brains. It's taken me a
18 long time to figure him out, but now that I have I'm really
19 ashamed of myself. John started having trouble keeping up
20 with his classes during football season. He was too busy
21 with football practices and lifting weights. He started
22 asking me if he could copy my homework. I felt funny
23 about it, but like I said, he's every girl's dream, so what
24 was I going to say? I gave him my homework.
25   As the school year went by I actually thought John
26 might ask me out. I thought if I kept letting him borrow my
27 work that maybe we'd really have something together,
28 something special. When our chemistry lab reports came
29 due, he borrowed my book for the weekend to copy it.
30 During tests he made sure he sat right behind me, so that

1   any chance he got he could see my answers.

2   If I could give John an award it would be for the Best
3   Cheater of the Year! And today, I watched while John
4   received more awards than I could even count. Between
5   his athletic awards and, believe it or not, his academic
6   awards, he was on the stage more than any other
7   student in my class.

8   John doesn't deserve any of the academic awards he
9   won. And without the good grades he earned through
10   cheating, he probably would have been kicked off the
11   athletic teams, too. He wouldn't have the thousands of
12   dollars in scholarship money he won.

13   The reason I feel terrible is ... because I'm just as
14   guilty as he is. I let him copy my work all year just
15   because I thought he might ask me out one day. What
16   an idiot I am! Why would I want to go out with someone
17   who was willing to cheat his way through every course
18   this year?

19   I guess there's nothing I can do about it now. I'm not
20   sure if I can ever forgive myself, though. There are lots
21   of students who should have won the awards John won.
22   I doubt if I'll ever go to a high school reunion in my life.
23   It's pretty ironic that I won the Citizenship Award, isn't
24   it?

What's Your Opinion?

What would you do if you were in this girl's position? Do you believe she should speak out and let someone know John cheated all year? Should she tell on herself? If she does speak out, what actions do you think the school should take? Should this young lady and John have to give up their awards? How would you react if a friend of yours came to you and asked you to let him/her copy your work or cheat from your paper on a test?

Most students don't think they're hurting anyone else when they're cheating. Explain how many students' lives were affected by this girl's actions.

A Broken Heart

1   If one more person calls me up and tells me they know
2 some guy they want me to meet, I'm going to scream!
3 Don't people understand I just don't want to go out with
4 anyone right now?

5   Josh and I had a great thing going. We went out for the
6 past year. Then, all of a sudden, out of the clear blue, he
7 decides he wants to be "free." He doesn't want to be "tied
8 down." He thinks we should get to know other people.

9   How could he do this to me? He promised me that he
10 loved me, and that he'd always be there for me. Take a
11 little advice from me, girls, when a guy tells you he "loves"
12 you, turn around and run as fast as you can in the opposite
13 direction.

14   My friends keep telling me that Josh will realize in a
15 few weeks how he made a mistake. They say he'll come
16 running back to me once he realizes what he's lost. If he
17 does, I don't know what I'll say. I don't understand how I
18 can still love him when he's hurt me so much ... but I do.

19   I think guys need to be more careful with the words
20 they say. I mean, don't even bring up the words, "I love
21 you," if you don't mean forever. Josh even talked about
22 getting married. We used to say that we'd have two kids
23 and live in a two-story house with a big porch.

24   I never dreamed he'd break up with me. I thought we
25 were forever. It's only been a week since we broke up, but
26 I've already lost five pounds. My stomach feels sick all the
27 time. No matter how hard I try I can't concentrate in class.
28 I failed two tests last week.

29   When I see Josh in the halls he hardly even notices me.
30 Just tell me how someone can change their feelings so

1 quickly. One week it's "I'll love you forever," and the
2 next, "We need to be apart. We're not good for each
3 other anymore."

4   For a long time Josh wanted to get physical … if you
5 know what I mean. Things had gotten pretty intense,
6 but I still wouldn't give in. I wonder if Josh and I would
7 still be together if we had "done it." Even though he
8 didn't say it, I think that's the real reason he broke up.
9 He's ready for a physical relationship, and I'm not.

10   But if I don't start feeling any better, I might change
11 my mind. The way I feel right now, I'd do anything to get
12 Josh back.

What's Your Opinion?

Do you feel teen-agers are too "free" with their words, saying "I love you" long before they really know if they're in love? Explain. How long do you think it takes to know if you're in love? If you're in love right now, when or how did you realize it?

It sounds like our actor truly loves Josh. What's your opinion about her becoming physically involved with him in order to get him back?

Accepting Death

1   Why is it that people have to die? I just don't get it. It
2 seems as if people who spend their entire life caring about
3 others should be allowed to live forever.

4   My grandmother died today. She was ninety-nine, and
5 I truly believed she would live forever. In my heart she still
6 does live on. There has to be more to this world than just
7 this, doesn't there? I have to believe she's in a heaven
8 someplace so special where she will always be healthy and
9 happy.

10   She told me not to grieve for her after she was gone.
11 She said that it was time for her to go to a much better
12 place, where she would never feel pain or heartache again.
13 I'm trying hard to do what she asked me to do, but it's so
14 hard. I miss her so much.

15   When I was little my sisters and I took turns staying
16 overnight at my grandma's apartment. I loved the licorice
17 candy she kept in her glass jar. It was wrapped in shiny
18 silver paper and brought out only for us.

19   We loved to sit and play Pick-Up Sticks with her.
20 Somehow I always won. When I became an adult and my
21 own children would play this game with Grandma, I
22 suddenly realized that Grandma always lets the children
23 win!

24   Grandma worked in a rescue mission house. She spent
25 her entire life helping people who were having hard times.
26 It was her religion that kept her brave, her belief that God
27 is real and that he was always with her. Everyone at the
28 mission respected my grandma. It doesn't seem right that
29 she's gone.

30   My whole outlook on life has changed now. When

1 Grandma was alive I didn't even think about death. It
2 was something I knew happened all around me, but
3 never to someone I knew. Now, I've learned to
4 appreciate every day I'm alive. We never know when it
5 will be our turn to pass on from this world.

6   Grandma's death taught me to look around for the
7 little things in life that can bring joy. I try to look for the
8 bright side of things. I used to be upset when I had to
9 go to work after school, now I'm thankful I have a job.
10 When a storm comes that ruins my plans, I know that
11 plans can be changed and the sun will eventually come
12 out again. When my mom and dad make rules I don't
13 like, at least I know they care about me.

14   It's funny how death changes a person. I feel like
15 Grandma is looking down on me from heaven, helping
16 me to understand that my life has a purpose, and it's my
17 responsibility to figure out what it is and do it.

18   *(The next line is said looking upward.)* I'm trying,
19 Grandma. I really am. I think I finally understand what
20 you meant when you said, "Life's not easy, but it is
21 worthwhile."

What's Your Opinion?

What does the phrase, "Life's not easy, but it is worthwhile,"
mean to you?

Have you figured out what your purpose in life is? Explain.
What talents do you possess? (I.e., music, athletics, patience,
etc.) How could you use your talents to touch other people?

The Prom – Who Thought Up Such a Stupid Idea?

1   Here it is already, the spring of my senior year.
2 Everyone is rushing around getting ready for the prom.
3 This year's theme is, "Some Enchanted Evening." Yeah,
4 right. I'll really be having "some enchanted evening"
5 sitting at home watching a movie.

6   I want to know, who thought up such a stupid idea as
7 the prom anyway? Or better yet, why do we still have a
8 prom? I mean, we're in the new millennium. The idea of a
9 prom is so archaic. Can't we come up with something new
10 to do?

11   You're probably thinking I don't have a date for the
12 prom and that's why I'm criticizing, right? The fact is three
13 girls asked me. My problem is not getting a date, it's
14 paying for everything!

15   It's not that my family is poor, but I work to help out.
16 I'd have to work a whole month to come up with enough
17 money to take a girl to the prom. Maybe if I had a special
18 girl I really wanted to take ... but to spend all that money
19 on "just a friend," it's too much.

20   I asked my mom what her prom was like. She said they
21 got dressed up in gowns and the guys rented tuxedos. The
22 girls got flowers, and if they were lucky, they got to take
23 one of their parents' cars to the dance.

24   Nowadays, kids rent limos and half of them get hotel
25 rooms to have parties in after the dance. How can I
26 compete with that? Where do they get all their money?

27   Some of my friends think I'm crazy. They ask me, "How
28 can you not go to your senior prom? It's like a tradition.

1   Everyone in the senior class goes to the prom."
2   Well, I think we should start a new tradition. Maybe
3   the prom committee should sponsor a worthwhile
4   charity. Every couple could donate half the money they
5   would spend on a fancy dress, or a tuxedo, limos,
6   parties and everything else they buy, to the charity.
7   Then, instead of buying such expensive clothes for the
8   dance, dress casual. Do you realize how much money
9   we'd raise?
10   I figure every couple going to the dance puts out
11   close to five hundred dollars easily. If you multiply that
12   by one hundred couples ... that's fifty-thousand dollars!
13   Imagine being able to donate half of that to something
14   worthwhile.
15   Oh well, in order to do that we'd have to turn the
16   entire senior class into unselfish, concerned and caring
17   citizens, and I don't see that happening anytime soon.
18   But instead of staying home and watching a movie the
19   night of prom, I think I just convinced myself to get out
20   and do something worthwhile. Do you want to join me?

What's Your Opinion?

How much does it cost a couple at your school to attend the prom? Do you feel students overspend? Explain. Share some ideas to save money on the cost to attend prom.

How do you feel about our narrator's idea of the class sponsoring a charity on prom night?

I Want to Quit!

1   When I was fifteen my mom told me I had outgrown her
2 pocketbook. As soon as I was sixteen I was to find a job. I
3 guess she was right. I wanted to go to the movies or
4 bowling every weekend, and afterwards we always went for
5 pizza. I also like clothes and shoes. Of course, I can't
6 forget makeup and getting my nails done. Oh yeah, I also
7 started tanning once a week at the tanning salon this year.

8   So, I agreed that I would get a job. I've been working
9 for three months now, and I hate it. I'm a cashier at the
10 local department store. It's the most boring thing someone
11 could be forced to do. One hour after another I stand
12 there, scanning items. On sale days half of the sale prices
13 don't come up and the customer gets mad at me. Don't
14 they know to always look for a UPC code before they pick
15 something up? Then people buy these fifty-pound bags of
16 dog food which I have to load into their cart. Every night
17 after work my neck and back are killing me.

18   Well, this week I had had enough. I told my mom that
19 I wanted to quit. To me, working is close to torture. I
20 mean, I'm only sixteen and I really don't think I should
21 have to work. I get straight A's in school, I do my own
22 laundry, and I keep my room spotless. Isn't that enough? I
23 feel like my parents want me to be this grown-up person
24 that I don't think I should have to be yet.

25   After I told my mom I wanted to quit, she said, "Fine,
26 quit if you want to, just go put a 'For Sale' sign on your
27 car." Imagine that, I have to sell my car if I want to quit
28 working. Mom said she and Dad can't afford the monthly
29 payment for my car on top of their cars. She also told me
30 that I wouldn't be allowed to drive her new van, I'd only be

1 allowed to drive my dad's old car.

2   This is really unfair, because Dad is out of town so
3 much that I'd hardly ever have a vehicle to drive. Right
4 now I don't really care whether I can keep my car or not,
5 because I only have my permit. I suppose once I have
6 my license it will make a difference. Mom said that
7 having my own car is one of my first tickets to having
8 some independence, that I just can't see that yet. She
9 thinks I should stop complaining about work and learn
10 to "grin and bear it," as she puts it.

11   I don't know what to do. Don't tell me to go find a
12 different job. While I truly hate my job, I don't think I
13 would like working at a fast-food restaurant any better,
14 and I know I don't like baby-sitting. What else am I
15 qualified to do? Nothing.

16   College is looking better and better all the time.

What's Your Opinion?

What suggestions could you give this teen about her job?
How else might she be able to earn money for all of her wants?
Do you think someone this young really needs all the things she
has?

Just how much do you think a parent should pay for beyond
food, clothing and shelter for their children? Explain.

S.A.D.D.

1   I always thought those clubs that preach "Don't drink
2 and drive" were so lame. I mean who wants to waste their
3 free time getting together to raise money for some
4 organization that is always getting down on kids for
5 drinking?

6   But lately, my feelings about the group have changed.
7 All it took was listening to this guy who spoke at school
8 yesterday. What I'm going to tell you is a true story about
9 some young people who caused a lot of sadness because
10 of alcohol.

11   This man, his name is Ron, told us a story about his
12 best friend, Mark. Ron and Mark were best friends since
13 grade school. They did everything together. The boys were
14 on the same Little League team, they joined football
15 together, they ate supper at each other's houses at least
16 three times a week, they even went out on their first date
17 together.

18   As they got older they played high school sports, and,
19 because they were both really good at football, they
20 decided to go to the same college together to continue
21 playing football. It was there they fell in love with two
22 young girls who were also best friends. Their lives seemed
23 perfect. Beautiful girlfriends, a great college football
24 career, life was good.

25   The day came, though, when Mark decided it was time
26 to get married. And while Ron was also in love, he decided
27 that this time, it was finally OK to *not* do something at the
28 same time as Mark! Naturally, Mark asked Ron to be his
29 best man.

30   The weekend of the big day arrived and everything was

1 wonderful. After the wedding rehearsal Ron and the
2 other groomsmen told Mark he had to go out with them
3 one last time as a single man. Mark didn't want to go.
4 He was tired and only wanted to go to bed and get a
5 good night's rest.
6   But Ron wouldn't take "no" for an answer. He talked
7 Mark into taking a ride into town to get some pizza at
8 the gang's old hangout. On the way to the pizza place,
9 a speeding car crashed head-on into Ron's car. There
10 was nothing he could do. One moment he and Mark
11 were reminiscing about the old days and how excited
12 Mark was about his future, and within seconds Mark's
13 life was over ... the night before his wedding.
14   The other car had a bunch of teenagers in it, the
15 same age as you and me. They'd been drinking and were
16 just out having some fun. Because of them, four people
17 were killed that night, and a young woman lost the man
18 she was going to marry just hours before her wedding.
19   I can't even imagine how terrible it would be to live
20 through something like that. Ron has vowed to spend
21 his life fighting drunk driving. After listening to his
22 story, I decided I needed to do what I could, too. I'm
23 going to join S.A.D.D. I wish you would. It only takes
24 one person at a time to make a difference.

What's Your Opinion?

What are some ways you can help prevent drunk driving?

When someone is arrested for drunk driving, what do you believe the consequence should be? Do you believe the laws against drunk drivers are strict enough? Explain.

A Few Minutes of Fun

1   Two months ago I was on top of the world. I was dating
2 a cheerleader, and I was the star quarterback on the
3 football team. It was like a dream come true. Take it from
4 me, my dream has turned into a nightmare. And worst of
5 all, it's my fault, my own stupid fault.

6   I started dating Jeannie last year. At first, everything
7 was cool. We went out with our friends, going places like
8 the movies, football and basketball games, hayrides ... you
9 know, all the things kids in high school do. It was great.

10   But after awhile, Jeannie started talking about love.
11 Sure, I liked Jeannie a lot. I wanted to be with her more
12 than any girl I had ever dated. But, love?

13   When Jeannie said those three words, "I love you," for
14 the first time it made me feel great. I mean, here she was,
15 one of the most popular girls in school telling me she loved
16 me. What else could I say back? I had to tell her I loved
17 her, too. Anything else would have sounded stupid. So, I
18 said it. I told her I loved her.

19   It wasn't long after that that Jeannie and I started
20 getting pretty physical with each other. I thought a lot
21 about what it would be like to be with her ... you know
22 what I mean. I could tell she was feeling the same way. I
23 should've been prepared. I knew where we were headed. I
24 could tell ... all I had to do was tell Jeannie I wanted her,
25 and I knew she would give herself to me.

26   But instead of being prepared for this, we just let it
27 happen. How stupid! We acted like two irresponsible
28 teenagers.

29   The football coach at the state university called
30 yesterday to offer me a four-year scholarship to college. A

1   free ride! I was never so happy. My family was thrilled.
2   My dad always hoped I would play college ball. He spent
3   hours with me when I was a little boy helping me learn
4   to pass the football.
5   The excitement lasted about one hour. That's when
6   Jeannie called to tell me the news ... she's pregnant.
7   She wants us to get married. She said her mom and dad
8   agree that getting married is the best choice. After all,
9   we'll be graduated before the baby arrives. Jeannie's
10   dad owns the hardware store in town, and he offered
11   me a job working at the store with him.
12   I am so confused. In just a few moments, I totally
13   messed up my life.
14   Telling your parents you're having a baby is
15   supposed to be an exciting time, right? Everyone's
16   supposed to be happy about the news. I'm scared to
17   death to tell my parents. I have no idea what to do.
18   I don't want to get married. I'm only eighteen. This
19   is crazy! There has to be another way.

What's Your Opinion?

What's your advice to this young man on how to handle his situation? How would you handle things if you were in the same position?

What can be done to stop teen pregnancy? Is it fair that so many young girls get pregnant, then expect their own parents to raise the child? What are your feelings about adoption?

Happily Ever After? Yeah, Right!

1   I guess it's time for my family to join the vast majority.
2 My parents just told me they're getting divorced. I can't
3 believe it! Well, actually, I can. I guess I always thought
4 they'd keep working things out. But the older you get, the
5 more you can tell when there's really not any love between
6 your mom and dad.

7   I have to wonder why people even get married anymore.
8 None of my friends' parents are still married. My friends
9 always said they wished they could have my parents
10 because they were the only couple they knew who were
11 married over twenty years.

12   How can two people split up after twenty-two years
13 together? My parents have always taught me to deal with
14 problems whenever a friend and I have a disagreement.
15 So, why can't they do the same thing?

16   One time I heard this lady on television talking about
17 troubled couples. I listened to her for awhile because I had
18 a feeling my parents were not getting along. She said these
19 couples should pull out their wedding pictures and stare at
20 them for awhile. Then she said that people should always
21 remember the way they felt on that special day, the reason
22 they chose to be together and to remember everything it
23 was about the other person that they loved.

24   That sounds pretty easy to me. I'm not stupid, though.
25 I know that lots of things change over the years. But I
26 thought people *promised* to stay together "through good
27 times and bad, through sickness and health, for richer or
28 poorer," and all that other stuff they say.

29 *(This is said with hope.)* **Maybe I should talk to my mom**
30 **and dad. I could pull out their pictures and ask them to**

1   look at them, to tell me why they fell in love with each
2   other. Then I could ask them to please give things one
3   more try, because I know that's what they'd want me to
4   do if it were me in their position. I'll tell them that
5   twenty-two years together is too long to just throw their
6   marriage away.
7   This might work. I could even cook a romantic
8   candlelight dinner for two. My dad loves roast beef with
9   potatoes and carrots, and my mom could sit and relax,
10   instead of worrying about the food. I can do this. It just
11   might work!
12   Hey, I know, just because it worked on *Parent Trap*
13   doesn't mean it will work for my family, but I have to at
14   least try. My parents quit trying; this is my last hope.

What's Your Opinion?

Do you feel children should interfere when parents are experiencing marriage difficulties? Explain. In your opinion is there anything wrong with what our actor is planning? Explain.

Tell what you think it takes to make a marriage last forever. What kind of a person are you looking for in order to make a lifelong commitment? If you don't plan to ever marry, explain why.

Grounded for Life!

1   My father is being absolutely ridiculous, not to mention
2 unfair! He grounded me for a whole week! Not only did he
3 ground me for a week, but to make things even worse this
4 is the last week of my summer vacation. On Monday school
5 starts!

6   He is over-reacting big time. I mean, I know I might
7 deserve to be punished for what I did a little bit, but being
8 grounded for a week does not equal the crime. I'll tell you
9 what I did, it was really no big deal. But, of course, Dad
10 thought it was.

11   On Friday night my parents were going to a wedding
12 reception. Mom asked me last week if I would baby-sit my
13 younger sister. I asked her to please get someone else
14 because this was the week of the county fair, and I knew
15 my boyfriend and I would want to go there. So, she got one
16 of her old students from school (my mom's a teacher) to
17 baby-sit.

18   Well, didn't my boyfriend call me at eight o'clock that
19 night to tell me he and his friends decided to make it a
20 "Guys' Night Out." I was really mad at him. I mean, I don't
21 care at all if he wants to go out with his friends sometimes,
22 but he could have let me know a little earlier so I could
23 make other plans, too.

24   Meanwhile, this other girl was already at our house
25 baby-sitting. I'm a couple years older than this girl, but I
26 decided to get to know her and try to make the best of the
27 night. We thought it would be more fun if my sister's friend
28 came over. Then we could have four of us, two baby sitters
29 and two kids. My sister liked the idea, so we called her
30 friend and she came over.

1   Next we did some stupid things. We just wanted to
2   have fun. I was already upset with my boyfriend and
3   then I was stuck at home for the night, so I thought we
4   could do some things to liven up the night. We decided
5   to take the little girls up on the roof of the house. I
6   didn't think it was that dangerous, I thought it would be
7   fun to watch the stars and sit up there talking. And it
8   was. The girls thought we were the coolest baby sitters
9   around.
10 After that we got into my mom's van, and I drove
11 everyone around the yard. I don't have my license, but
12 my mom has let me drive around empty parking lots.
13 Everyone was laughing and had a great time.
14 Things would have been cool if my little sister hadn't
15 blabbed about everything to my parents when they got
16 home. My dad flipped out. He said I was completely
17 irresponsible to do those things when I was the oldest in
18 charge. He asked me if I even stopped to think what
19 could have happened if someone had fallen off the roof,
20 or if I accidentally ran the van through the garage door.
21 I think he's going a little extreme here, but I guess he's
22 a little bit right. He was also mad that we invited over
23 another child to the house when he and Mom weren't
24 home.
25 I don't know why they're so upset. No one got hurt.
26 And why are they only mad at me? It's not like I forced
27 my little sister to go on the roof or get in the van. She
28 does have a mind of her own. But no, I'm the only one
29 to get in trouble. And what about the other girl baby-
30 sitting? My mom didn't say a word to her. She just said
31 she probably won't call her to baby-sit again.
32 Like I said, I don't mind being grounded for a day or
33 something, but a week? This is definitely unfair. What a
34 way to end my summer vacation.

What's Your Opinion?

What are some things you could do with children when you're baby-sitting which would be fun for you and the children, but not dangerous? Would you do the things our actor did? Do you feel only he/she should be punished for their actions? Explain.

If you were in this actor's position, what punishment, if any, do you believe is fair?

R-rated Movies – What's the Big Deal?

1 This past weekend I finally did something I knew I
2 wasn't allowed to do, but I did it anyway. I went into an
3 R-rated movie with some of my older friends. I know to
4 some of you that's no big deal, because I know that
5 everyone my age is allowed to go see them. It's just my
6 *parents* don't understand this.

7 I'm fifteen years old. Actually I'll be sixteen in three
8 months. So, I'm almost old enough to go. My parents said
9 that when I'm seventeen, they would rather I not see R-rated
10 shows, but that it will be my choice.

11 I keep trying to tell them that what I see on television
12 is nearly as bad as an R-rated movie. My mom says that
13 might be almost true for some of the movies, but for a lot
14 of them she disagrees. She says that when the movies
15 come out on video, and she watches them first to make
16 sure there's nothing really bad on it, then I can watch it. I
17 guess that's true, because she has let me watch two or
18 three that she had already seen.

19 It's just that everyone else is allowed to go to the
20 theatre and see them. When I'm with them they keep
21 pressuring me to go in. They say that no one will ever
22 know and to just tell my parents I saw something else.

23 That's easy for them to say, because they don't have
24 my mother asking all kinds of questions about the movie
25 when they get home. I think my mom knows my friends do
26 this to me, and she tries to figure out if I gave in and did
27 what they said or if I followed my parents' rule.

28 Well, Friday night my friends and I met some guys at

1 the movies. Everyone wanted to go to the R-rated movie
2 showing. Imagine how stupid I would have felt if I spoke
3 up and said, "Sorry guys, but I'm not allowed to go. I
4 have to go to PG-13." I couldn't do it. I had to go in with
5 them.
6   But to tell you the truth, I thought the movie was
7 really stupid, and now I feel guilty because I lied to my
8 mom and dad. I'm not sure it was worth it.

What's Your Opinion?

How do you feel about students under seventeen viewing R-rated movies? Compare R-rated shows to movies on television. Do you see R-rated movies and at what age do you believe it is appropriate for students to see them?

Should this student feel guilty about what she did? What would you have done if you were in a similar position? If you were allowed to see R-rated shows and your friend was not, would you be willing to go to a different movie rather than ask your friend to do something you know they're not allowed to do, or would you pressure them to come with you?

Cruisin'

1   It's only ten days until my birthday! Finally! I'll be
2 sixteen. I'm going *that* day to get my driver's permit. I
3 have been waiting for as long as I can remember to start
4 driving.

5   When I was twelve my dad taught me to drive our
6 riding lawn mower. I thought I was so cool out there
7 whipping around the yard on the mower. Not only did I get
8 to pretend I was driving, I got paid and a suntan besides!

9   You would think after all those years of driving the
10 mower, four long years to be exact, that my parents would
11 realize how ready I am to get behind the wheel of a car. For
12 some reason they don't trust me to drive!

13   When I questioned my dad he said, *(Change voice to*
14 *imitate father)* "Well, let's see, maybe it has something to do
15 with the time you failed to turn the lawn mower quickly
16 enough and put it into the field. The mower was stuck so
17 deep in the mud I had to call a tow truck."

18   I told him that was a long time ago, I mean a really long
19 time ago.

20   He answered me by saying, "Well, then, maybe it was
21 the time you were trying to get as close as possible to the
22 gas meter and you backed the mower into the meter and
23 dented the rear fender of the mower so badly it was stuck
24 in the tire."

25   When he said this to me I couldn't believe how unfair
26 he was being. I thought people were supposed to forgive
27 and forget each other's mistakes. How many times do I
28 have to apologize for those little accidents before my
29 parents will let me learn to drive?

30   Then he did the worst. He had to bring it up ... again.

1 He said, "Another reason may be that I can't quit
2 thinking of Dum-Dum, that's our old cat, flopping
3 around on the grass when you somehow managed to hit
4 him!"
5   I reminded Dad that he never liked the cat anyway,
6 and if I recall correctly, he told me I did everyone in the
7 family a favor when I ran over Dum-Dum.
8   It is with great seriousness I say to you that all of
9 these terrible things happened during the first two years
10 of driving the mower. I haven't had an accident for the
11 past two years. It seems funny to me that my parents
12 won't let me try to drive a car, but those little accidents
13 never stopped them from letting me drive the mower. As
14 long as I was saving my parents from having to do the
15 grass-cutting, my driving was good enough.
16   For some reason, this whole situation doesn't seem
17 fair. Does it sound fair to you? I've got to convince my
18 parents to let me drive. Maybe I should go on strike as
19 far as the grass-cutting goes. If I'm not allowed to drive
20 a car, then I guess I don't need to cut the grass. Maybe
21 that will make them change their minds.

What's Your Opinion?

If you were trying to convince your parents to teach you how to drive, what reasons would you give them to support your request? What types of arguments tend to arise between parents and teenagers when the teens begin driving?

Share your opinion on rules you believe are fair when sharing the car with your parents (i.e., paying for gas, how often you may use the car, etc.)

If you were our actor's parents, would you feel your teen was ready to learn to drive? Tell why you answered yes or no.

My Parents Are Dating!

1   I am really tired of the "dating scene." Oh ... don't be
2   confused. I'm not talking about *my* "dating scene." I'm
3   talking about my parents'! They've been divorced for about
4   a year now, and just recently they started dating again.
5   Oh, ... they're not dating each other. I mean other people,
6   of course.

7   The first guy my mom brought home was a class-A jerk.
8   He was this little short Italian guy. I guess he had plenty of
9   money, which is good, but I could tell the first time I met
10   him that he was a player. I mean, I knew he wasn't anyone
11   my mom should waste her time on. I didn't tell her that. I
12   guess he did make her laugh again, which I hadn't seen her
13   do much since the divorce. But, I had a feeling he was the
14   kind of guy who would never be satisfied with one woman.

15   Boy, was I right. My mom just happened to see him out
16   with another woman at this fancy restaurant in the city. He
17   had led Mom to believe she was the only one for him. What
18   a line. I couldn't believe my mom had the nerve to do this,
19   but I guess she actually walked up to the table where this
20   guy and the other woman were sitting and poured the
21   guy's glass of wine down the front of him! When she told
22   me this I busted up laughing. It was hilarious!

23   The thing that bothers me is that it's weird talking to
24   my mom about her boyfriends. I mean, isn't that supposed
25   to be *her* job, talking to me about my boyfriends? Ever
26   since she started dating again, I feel as if I'm the mother
27   and she's the child.

28   Then there's my dad. I'm not sure where he meets
29   some of these ladies he takes out. The one that's tagging
30   along with him now is a strange one. I've never seen her in

1   any color but black. Hey, I understand black is sexy, but
2   come on, every date? She wears her hair in this poofy
3   1950s style. It's probably the style she wore in her high
4   school days and she's never changed it. Oh, but the
5   best, or should I say the worst, fashion emergency she
6   has going are her shoes. These things have points on
7   them that could, as my sisters and I say, "kill a cricket
8   in the corner!" I get the feeling my dad is getting wise to
9   her, though. She's obviously after his money, and he
10   seems to be figuring that out. Thank goodness!

11   You might think I'm being really unfair or maybe too
12   critical of these people my parents are dating. It's not as
13   if I'm living a fantasy of my parents ever getting back
14   together or anything. I know that's never going to
15   happen. But couldn't they find someone to date that's at
16   least somewhat normal? Is that too much to ask?

17   I was talking to one of my teachers about this, and
18   she said that her parents were divorced and remarried.
19   She said that while it wasn't fun for her family to go
20   through, she feels like she has two sets of parents. She
21   really loves her stepparents as if they were her own.

22   That's what I'm hoping for, that my parents meet
23   new people who make them happy again ... and me, too.
24   Maybe I should write up a singles ad for my mom and
25   dad, you know, like they do in the newspaper. Hey, it
26   works in the movies. What do you think?

What's Your Opinion?

How would you feel about your parents dating? Maybe you've already experienced this. Share how this makes you feel. If you haven't experienced this, tell how you think you would feel.

Should parents wait to date after divorce until their children are grown?

Do you think our narrator should write a singles ad for her parents? Would you want to help your parents find someone to date if they were single? (Remember, if things get serious, these people could become your stepparents, and if they have children, you could suddenly find yourself with stepbrothers or stepsisters.) Or is this their business and the children should stay out of it?

I Have Got to Get Some Wheels!

1   If I don't get my own car pretty soon I'm going to go
2 crazy! My mother will only let me borrow her car to drive
3 to work and to go out one night a week. I'd buy my own
4 car if I could afford it, but there's no way I can.

5   I asked my parents to give me some help, but they feel
6 I should pay for the whole deal myself. I even suggested we
7 make it a loan, and I'd pay everything back. They said it
8 won't hurt me to wait awhile for a car, at least as long as
9 it takes for me to save up the money for one.

10   Why is it that I have to have the only parents, out of all
11 my friends, who think I should pay for everything? Some of
12 my friends got cars for their sixteenth birthdays, and some
13 of my friends only had to pay half of the cost. My parents
14 not only think I should pay for the whole car, but also the
15 car insurance and all the gas to put in it! Give me a break!

16   I tried explaining to Mom how much help I could be to
17 her. She's always complaining about how all she ever gets
18 done is driving us kids all over the countryside. She's even
19 nicknamed her car "Mama Leone's Taxi." But when I tried
20 convincing her, she said she really doesn't mind running us
21 everywhere. I ask myself, "Why do I have to listen to her
22 complain about it all the time then?"

23   Dad is just as tough. I explained to him that I could do
24 all the late-night pick-ups that he hates to do. You know,
25 like running out at 10:30 p.m. to buy milk, bread and all
26 those other things families run out of when you need them
27 most. But he claims that doesn't happen very often. I'm
28 going to start keeping track of how often it happens
29 because I know it happens at least three times a week!

30   I don't know. Maybe it's not even worth it. Dad told

1   me that even if I do save up enough money to buy my
2   own car, pay the insurance and put gas in it, I still have
3   to ride the bus to school. Can you believe it?! Dad says,
4   "Why drive when you have bus transportation that I pay
5   for with my tax dollars?"
6   My parents and I have a serious generational thing
7   going on, and right now, there doesn't seem to be a
8   thing I can do about it.

What's Your Opinion?

Share your own situation on owning a car. Sample questions you may wish to answer in your essay are: Do your parents allow you to own a car? How will it be paid for? What expenses do you feel you should have to pay for a car? If you own a car, do you feel you should have your own freedom to drive it where and when you want?

You may have your own ideas regarding this topic. Feel free to write about those, too.

Organ Donation – Should I?

1   It's weird to think about death, I guess that's
2   something we teenagers don't really worry about much. I
3   mean, as long as we're healthy we shouldn't have to worry
4   about it for at least another fifty years, I hope. But, I got
5   my driver's license today, and the lady there asked me
6   whether or not I wanted to be listed as an organ donor. So,
7   suddenly, I was faced with the reality that one day, I'll die.

8   It's hard to even think about death. It's not like it's
9   something you can try once to get over your fears, so that
10 the next time you do it you won't be afraid. There is no
11 next time. It happens, and you don't ever do it again.
12 Maybe that's why it's scary to me.

13 I asked my dad once if he was afraid to die. He said he
14 really wasn't. Dad says he considers dying simply a
15 transition from one type of life to another. Thinking of it
16 that way makes it not sound so scary, or so final.

17 But when that lady asked me about donating my
18 organs, I didn't know what to say. As I stood in line looking
19 back at her with my mouth hanging open, saying nothing,
20 another lady spoke up. She said, "Honey, you do what you
21 want to do, but the way I figure is, if I can help someone
22 else to live after I've already died, then in a strange way,
23 my spirit will live on through them. Do you understand
24 what I'm saying?"

25 I kind of shook my head a little, but I still didn't speak.
26 The man behind me added, "My nephew is living because
27 of a person willing to donate their organs. He was waiting
28 for nearly a year for a heart. We thought we were going to
29 lose him, but sure enough, some kind soul who was killed
30 in an automobile accident, donated his organs. Because of

1 that person, my nephew is living a normal life. As a
2 matter of fact, he's getting married this Saturday."
3   Suddenly the importance of organ donation struck
4 home. This man was talking about someone close to my
5 age, not some old person who would die in a few years
6 anyway.
7   Quickly, I looked up at the clerk, before I could
8 change my mind, and said, "Mark me as an organ
9 donor, please."
10   When I got home I told my parents what I had done.
11 You see, even if you note "Organ Donor" on your
12 license, your family can choose to not honor your
13 request when you die. I wanted them to know that if
14 anything happened to me, organ donation was my
15 wish. Mom and Dad both got tears in their eyes and told
16 me how much they prayed they would never have to
17 carry out my wishes, but ... if the time ever came they
18 would do as I asked.
19   I'm sure a lot of you are learning to drive, or maybe
20 already do. I hope you made the same choice I did.
21 Would you please list "Organ Donor" on your license?
22 Just think about it.

What's Your Opinion?

How do you feel about organ donation? Share your reasons for either being an organ donor, or choosing not to be a donor.

Organs removed after one's death are not always placed in the body of another human being. Sometimes they are donated to science for experimental use and study. How would you feel about that? Explain.

Sometimes It's Hard to Say "I'm Sorry"

1   I am really nervous right now. Sometime within the
2 next half hour I have to call one of my friend's mothers and
3 tell her I'm sorry for something I didn't do. My dad is
4 making me. Everyone seems like they're ganging up on me.
5 Even my friend seemed a little upset with me, even though
6 she agreed this wasn't my fault. Let me tell you what
7 happened. Maybe then I'll have another person on my side.

8   About a year ago my friend, her name is Emily, invited
9 me over to hang out. Emily's mom had rented a video
10 camera for the weekend because it was Emily's little
11 sister's birthday. When we saw the camera we couldn't
12 resist. We wanted to have some fun, so we filmed ourselves
13 doing these crazy commercials. They were hysterical! Even
14 Emily's mom said they were good enough for *Saturday*
15 *Night Live*.

16   Emily does this one face, kind've like this, *(Make a crazy*
17 *face)* and then she talks in this stupid voice, like this: *(Make*
18 *the face and talk in a funny voice while saying)* "**Hello, how is**
19 **everybody? My name is Emily. What's yours?**"

20   See what I mean? It's really funny when Emily does it.
21 Well, anyway, we recorded these commercials on the same
22 tape as Emily's sister's birthday party. We didn't tape over
23 anything, but Emily's mom wasn't too happy about the
24 commercials being on the same tape. I guess we should've
25 asked for a different tape. We just didn't think about it. It
26 really didn't seem like that big of a deal to us. Well, let me
27 tell you what happened next.

28   Last month, when my sister and I were bored, I thought

1   of that goofy tape Emily and I made. So, I called Emily
2   and asked her if we could borrow the tape. I knew it
3   would give my sister and me a good laugh, and like I
4   said, we were really bored.
5   When I went to pick up the tape, Emily's mom came
6   out with it. She handed it to me and said, "I'm very
7   nervous about loaning this to you, Steph. Remember,
8   Shawna's birthday party is on this. I don't want anything
9   to happen to this tape. It's very special to me."
10   I said, "Don't worry, Mrs. Shaffer. You don't have
11 anything to worry about. We'll be careful with it. I'll
12 bring it back tomorrow. Thanks!"
13   And that was that. My sister and I watched the tape
14 and laughed and laughed. Then I put it on the shelf, with
15 every intention of returning it to Mrs. Shaffer the next
16 day. But ... I forgot. It wasn't until a few weeks later
17 that Mrs. Shaffer called up to my house looking for the
18 tape, that I remembered.
19   Here's where the problem comes. I guess my sister
20 accidentally taped over Shawna's birthday party when
21 she was recording Jay Leno one night. Emily told me
22 about it at school, how her mother cried for two nights
23 over it. Emily said she thought I should call her mother
24 and apologize.
25   Well, I didn't do it! My sister did! And if anyone
26 should have to apologize it should be her, not me!
27 That's what I told Emily, which she told her mother. Can
28 you believe her mother actually called my father and
29 told him she felt I owed her an apology? She knows my
30 sister is the one who recorded over the birthday party,
31 but she said I was the one she gave responsibility to for
32 the tape.
33   So here I am, trying to think of what to say, when I
34 don't really think I should have to make this call
35 anyway. What would you say?

What's Your Opinion?

Do you believe Steph should have to call Mrs. Shaffer and apologize? If you were in Steph's place, what would you say? Should Steph's sister be included in the conversation? What do you think your parents would make you do in this same situation?

Have you ever been in a position where you owed someone an apology you found very difficult to admit you owed? Share your experience.

Vacation Blues

1   It's that time of year again, you know, the "quality
2 time" family vacation thing. This year we're going to the
3 shore. I used to really look forward to our trips to the
4 beach, but not this year.

5   We haven't been to the beach in three years, and
6 during that three years lots of things have changed. Let's
7 see, Mom and Dad decided to have a baby, and if that
8 wasn't bad enough, guess what? Mom had — twins! It is so
9 humiliating to be a teenager and have your mother still
10 giving birth. I don't even want to go there.

11   Anyway, can you imagine going to the shore with two-
12 year-old twin boys? Sounds like a lot of fun, huh? Yeah,
13 right. It sounds like lots of crying and temper tantrums to
14 me.

15   Well, I figured I'd try and make the best of it. So, I
16 came up with a plan. I asked Mom and Dad if I could bring
17 one of my friends along. Of course, she would have to pay
18 money towards the trip. I don't expect Mom and Dad to
19 pay for my friend. I presented all the reasons why this was
20 a good idea, but my parents still said, "No."

21   I do not understand them. I asked them to put
22 themselves in my place and see how they would feel. They
23 both tried to convince me that they would have been so
24 thrilled as teenagers just to get to go to the beach. In fact,
25 my parents claim that neither one of them ever got to take
26 a family vacation while they were growing up. I'm going to
27 ask my grandparents about that, because that's hard to
28 believe.

29   They want this to be a "family only" trip. Meanwhile,
30 all my friends are allowed to take a friend with them on

1   vacation. Some of their parents even pay all the
2   expenses for the extra person. I'm not even asking my
3   parents to do that!
4   Here are all the reasons I think my parents should
5   let my friend come with us:
6   One: I won't be grumpy because I don't have anyone
7   to talk to.
8   Two: I'll have someone to walk on the boardwalk
9   with.
10   Three: My friend and I could baby-sit *one* night, so
11 that Mom and Dad can go out for a quiet, romantic
12 dinner.
13   Four: We could wash the dishes after supper *every*
14 night. (Now I think that's really being generous, don't
15 you?)
16   Five: Now this one I didn't tell my parents, but I'll
17 have a lot better chance to meet a cute guy if I have a
18 friend with me, right? Guys usually hang out with
19 friends.
20   I would like to know if you have any suggestions to
21 help me convince my parents. Lots of kids are allowed
22 to take their friends on vacation, so tell me, how do they
23 do it?

What's Your Opinion?

What are your feelings on taking friends along on family
vacations? Have you ever invited a friend, or been the invited
guests on a vacation? If you said yes to either of these, share how
the vacation went.

What suggestions could you give our actor to help her
convince her parents hers is a good idea?

Try and see this situation from her parents' perspective. Tell
why you think these parents don't want to budge on their
decision.

Don't Take Anything for Granted

1   I am not the same person now that I was three weeks
2 ago. You might ask, how could a person change that much
3 in only three weeks? I know it sounds crazy, but believe
4 me, it's true.

5   A few months ago, my church announced plans to take
6 a mission trip to Mexico. I have always wanted to travel to
7 Mexico, so this sounded like a dream come true for me.
8 Under any other circumstances I knew my parents
9 wouldn't allow me to travel so far away, but if I was going
10 with the church group, well ... that would be OK. So, I
11 signed up.

12   Boy, was I in for a surprise. My idea of Mexico was
13 beautiful sandy beaches, the sun shining every day and a
14 chance to practice the little bit of Spanish I learned this
15 year in school. I also thought I might meet a gorgeous
16 dark-skinned *muchacho,* (Muchacha, if a boy is delivering this
17 monolog) if you know what I mean.

18   Well, the first morning I was in Mexico, our counselors
19 had us out of bed before the sun was up. Now I'm sorry,
20 but I have always felt that a person should never have to
21 wake up before the sun. Don't you agree?

22   My friends and I ran a day camp for young children. I
23 guess I was expecting the children to look like the kids I
24 taught at bible school last year back in the states. You
25 know, little girls with ponytails that are tied up by ribbons
26 that match their shorts, and the little boys wearing ball
27 caps with their favorite professional baseball team logo on
28 the front.

29   Believe me, what I saw on the first day of day camp
30 made my heart break. These children were so poor most of

1   them didn't wear shoes. Their clothes were dirty and
2   patched. The first thing we did was scrub the children's
3   hands and faces. We brushed their hair, and I even put
4   pretty ribbons in the little girls' hair. If you could have
5   seen the smiles on those children's faces when they saw
6   themselves in a mirror with clean skin and pretty-smelling
7   hair ... it's hard to put into words how it made me feel.
8   During the first art activity I realized how special and
9   appreciative these children were. I brought along a large
10 bag of broken pieces of crayons my little brother was
11 throwing away. As I passed a crayon to each child and
12 told them it was theirs to keep, their eyes popped open
13 so wide, like they might never shut again. You'd have
14 thought I handed them a piece of gold, but instead it
15 was just a broken piece of crayon.
16   In my school if the teacher hands out paper, and
17 someone gets a piece with a little crinkle in it, they want
18 a new piece of paper. Or if they start drawing and make
19 a mistake, they throw the paper away. The teacher has
20 to make them turn the paper over and use the other
21 side.
22   Not the kids in Mexico. They *wanted* to draw on
23 both sides of the paper. Some of the children even drew
24 really small pictures so they wouldn't use up the whole
25 sheet of paper. They wanted to have some paper left
26 over for another day!
27   I used to be embarrassed by the small trailer my
28 family lives in. Not anymore. After seeing the places
29 those children sleep in night after night, my trailer looks
30 like a palace.
31   When I was really little my mother would get mad
32 when I didn't eat all of my supper. She'd say, "There are
33 children in the world who are starving and you're
34 throwing all that good food away." Now I know what she
35 meant. *(Pause)* Nowadays, I even eat my peas.

What's Your Opinion?

Share ways in which you believe our country takes its riches for granted. What can you do to change these attitudes?

Would you be interested in traveling to a foreign country on a mission trip? (It doesn't have to be a religious trip; there are Peace Corps groups, etc.) Tell why or why not.

A Moral Judgment

1   I am so angry right now I can hardly speak, I just want
2 to yell! I can't believe how my school has hurt my best
3 friend. She has been through so much already this year,
4 and now this is the worst!

5   You see, during the summer, my best friend, Chelsey,
6 got pregnant. I agree that getting pregnant was not exactly
7 the smartest thing to do, but ... she's certainly not the first
8 person this has happened to nor the last. And it's not as if
9 the father of her baby was someone Chelsey just met and
10 had a one-night stand with. She and her boyfriend have
11 been together for three years.

12   Up until summer, though, Chelsey was a straight-A
13 student. She never talks back to the teachers and everyone
14 likes her. She's been my best friend since first grade, and
15 I don't ever remember her being mean to anyone, she
16 won't even kill a bug!

17   Chelsey decided she wanted to keep her baby. She
18 knew how much work the baby would be, but her family is
19 great and everyone is helping her as much as they can.
20 Chelsey comes to school until one o'clock every day, then
21 she's able to leave to go home and take care of the baby.
22 Her boyfriend is also on an adjusted work release
23 schedule. He leaves school at noon and goes to work at the
24 local K-Mart. He's also helping her as much as he can.
25 They want to get married after they graduate in June.

26   Yes, it's great that the school helped both of them by
27 giving them special schedules, but ... the school sure let
28 Chelsey down, too. This past week students were
29 nominated for National Honor Society. Right now Chelsey
30 is ranked fifth in our entire class. Despite everything she's

1   been through, she's been able to stay on top. I think
2   that's deserving of being in National Honor Society,
3   don't you?
4   Well, the school didn't think so. I guess part of the
5   description of a Society member is the person must be
6   of good moral character. The school decided that since
7   Chelsey had a baby before she was married that she no
8   longer qualifies as a good moral person. Would they
9   rather she had an abortion!
10   I'm sorry, but I can't keep quiet about this. I hope my
11   parents understand how I feel because I'm going to the
12   principal, no ... better yet, I'll go to the superintendent.
13   *(Pauses to think a minute.)* Even better yet, I'm going to
14   the newspaper. I'm sure the local women's shelters and
15   other organizations who believe in women's rights will
16   help.
17   I've just got to get Chelsey in National Honor
18   Society. It's not even so much the idea of being in the
19   Society, it's the idea that Chelsey needs her self-worth
20   back, because right now, they've taken it away.

What's Your Opinion?

What type of person do you believe should be accepted into your school's National Honor Society? Do you feel Chelsey should still be a member even though she had a baby out of wedlock? Why or why not?

If you were Chelsey's friend, how would you help her?

What Is a Family?

1   I'm getting pretty sick and tired of things around my
2 house lately. Let me tell you everything my mother made
3 me do just this week.

4   First of all, Mom needed to go grocery shopping, so
5 she asked me to baby-sit my baby brother and sister. Mom
6 says she always spends more when she takes them with
7 her, because she can't stand them pitching a fit in front of
8 everybody. She ends up buying lollipops and sugar-coated
9 cereal just to make the twins happy.

10   Now, understand, I don't get paid to baby-sit. Mom
11 says it's something I should do just because I'm a part of
12 the family, and I need to help the family. I don't think
13 that's fair. I didn't choose to have two more kids, my mom
14 did. Why shouldn't she baby-sit them? Anyway, I think I
15 should at least get paid when I watch them. I certainly
16 work hard enough when I baby-sit them. Have you ever had
17 to change two diapers on two screaming kids, at one time?

18   Well, that's just the beginning. Mom actually made me
19 wash the dishes every night this week. She said that she
20 cooks the meals, so I can help her by cleaning them up. I
21 swear she purposely cooked greasy meat, because she
22 knows I hate greasy meat. All those pans with that excess
23 fat floating in the grease made me want to throw up. I even
24 wore rubber gloves practically up to my shoulders, and I
25 still got grease in my nails. There must have been a leak in
26 one of the gloves.

27   I told my mother it wasn't fair I had to clean up after
28 five people. I said I was more than willing to wash the
29 dishes I used, but it wasn't right that I had to wash every
30 single person's dishes in my family.

1   Mom said when you're part of a family you have to
2   all pitch in to help each other. She said this was one
3   more way I could really make her life easier.
4   What about my life? I didn't have any say-so in this
5   definition of what she thinks a family is. I'll tell you what
6   I think a family is.
7   A family should always be happy and get along.
8   There shouldn't be any fighting or yelling at each other.
9   Each person should take care of themselves. No one
10 should have to clean up after the other people, or baby-
11 sit younger brothers and sisters. A family should have
12 fun doing things together, but if you'd rather be with
13 your friends than your family, then that should be OK,
14 too.
15   When I grow up that's what my family is going to be
16 like.

What's Your Opinion?

Share your opinion on what a family is. Also, share your ideas on the subject of baby-sitting younger brothers and sisters, helping out with chores around the house, and spending time with friends rather than family.

Why Do People Change?

1   Rick has been my best friend since preschool. We were
2 always so much alike. Anywhere a person saw Rick, I'd be
3 right beside him. Our parents used to joke that if they
4 didn't know better, they'd guess we were really twins,
5 separated at birth.

6   Rick's favorite football team is the Steelers, so is mine.
7 He likes to eat cold pizza for breakfast. Of course, I do,
8 too. One time we even liked the same girl. That didn't work
9 out too well, though. We finally agreed that neither one of
10 us wanted to go out with her if it meant messing up our
11 friendship.

12   But lately, Rick has changed. I'm so mad at him right
13 now I don't know what to do. Last Friday night we were
14 invited to this party. Rick and I had already made plans to
15 go to the movies with some friends from another school.
16 We decided we'd go to the party for awhile, and later meet
17 our friends at the theatre.

18   The party was a lot of fun ... at first. Then I started to
19 notice some real "dead heads" arriving. I was glad we had
20 a reason to leave the party early. I started looking around
21 for Rick, so we could head out. When I finally saw him he
22 was standing with a gang of kids who call themselves,
23 "Trouble."

24   I waved at Rick and he waved back. He didn't seem to
25 understand, I was trying to tell him that we needed to
26 leave. Finally, I walked over to him and grabbed his arm,
27 not hard or anything, just enough to let him know we were
28 in a hurry. I said, "Let's go, Rick. The movie starts in
29 twenty minutes."

30   He looked at me in a way that said he didn't know what

1   I was talking about. I said, "Remember, we're meeting
2   our friends at the movies? We need to go, now."
3   Then I realized why Rick didn't know what was
4   going on. He was drinking! The next thing I knew some
5   strange-looking creature with earrings stuck in his nose,
6   eyebrow and tongue came asking Rick for money. Rick
7   pulled some out and said, "There's my share, right? Ten
8   bucks?"
9   Rick was putting in beer money. That was it. I was
10   disgusted with him. I turned around and left Rick at the
11   party. *(Pause)*
12   I thought I was mad then, but the next day was
13   worse. Rick's mom was visiting my mom. She told my
14   mom how bad Rick felt that I left him at the party and
15   went to the movies without him just because he wanted
16   to talk to one of his friends for a few minutes. She
17   wondered if something was bothering *me*. So, my mom
18   asked me what my problem was.
19   What I should do is tell on Rick, but then I'd feel like
20   we were in grade school or something. Even though I'm
21   mad at him, he's still my friend.
22   I don't know why people always have to change.
23   Why can't everyone just stay the same? I can't believe
24   my best friend is messed up.

What's Your Opinion?

Have you ever had a best friend who changed in a way which caused your friendship to be affected? Why do you think friendships, at times, grow apart? Rick not only had changed and was drinking, but he lied to his mother about his friend. How would you handle the situation presented in our monolog?

Nobody Has to Be Home by Ten-thirty!

1   OK, I'm going to ask your opinion about something
2 that has been bugging me for the past month. On the
3 weekends my friends and I like to go do things. Mostly we
4 go to the movies and get something to eat. My problem is
5 that my mother and father say I have to be home by ten-
6 thirty. That's right, ten-thirty! You probably can't believe it
7 either, right?

8   I tried to explain to my parents that by the time we eat,
9 and then go to the nine o'clock show it's impossible to be
10 home by ten-thirty! Most of my friends don't have to be in
11 until at least eleven-fifteen. That way they have time to see
12 the late show and still be home by curfew.

13   Well, my mom has a solution to everything. When I
14 tried to explain to her why I need a later curfew she said,
15 "All you need to do is start your evening earlier. Instead of
16 going out at seven o'clock to eat and then to a nine o'clock
17 show, go to eat at five and the show at seven. You'll make
18 your curfew with an hour to spare!"

19   I said, "Mom! I could never be ready to go out to eat
20 by five o'clock. I don't even get off the bus until four. That
21 hardly gives me enough time to shower and get dressed,
22 besides fixing my hair. That plan would never work."

23   My mom told me I could win an Academy Award for my
24 dramatic skills. Then she said, " I guess you'll just have to
25 learn to get ready faster. Of course, there's always a
26 second option ... you could stay home with Daddy and me."

27   You have to understand, my parents are really into
28 "family time." Mom says that with an earlier curfew we can

1   **both be happy — I get to see my friends, and I'm still**
2   **home early enough for my dad and her to see me for**
3   **awhile.**
4   **I don't get it. I mean, I'm a very responsible person.**
5   **And it's not like we live in a huge city. Nothing ever**
6   **happens in our town. What are my parents so uptight**
7   **about? All I want is an extra forty-five minutes. Is that**
8   **really too much to ask?**

What's Your Opinion?

Do you feel parents should have curfews for their teenagers? Explain. When should curfews be changed? Should you be in at different times for different nights of the week? Does where you live make a difference as to what your curfew should be? Tell why or why not.

In some cities and towns parents don't even have to give curfews because the local authorities do it for them. Why do you think they do this? Is it a good idea?

On Harassment

1   Yesterday I was walking down the hall when this guy in
2   my class started walking really close behind me. I turned
3   around and told him to back off. Instead of leaving me
4   alone, he laughed and got even closer to me. I warned him
5   again to get away from me.

6   I guess he thought he was really all that, because he
7   moved even closer, so close I could feel his belt buckle
8   rubbing up against the back of me. I was furious. I yelled
9   at him again to get away from me, but he just kept walking
10   as close as possible to me. I did the only thing left to do, I
11   turned around and smacked him right across the mouth.

12   When I got home I told my mom about what happened.
13   She asked me if I got in trouble for hitting the kid. There
14   weren't any teachers in the hall to see, so I didn't. I was
15   glad when she told me that really I should have told an
16   adult about what was going on and not hit the kid, but that
17   she didn't care that I did. She said that what he was doing
18   was trying to make me feel powerless and frightened, and
19   she was proud that I handled things on my own.

20   I have to tell you, that kid hasn't bothered me since. I
21   knew he wouldn't tell anyone what happened, because he
22   knows he'd be in more trouble than me. I guess I just don't
23   understand why guys get a big kick out of making girls feel
24   stupid. One of my friends said the guy who did this likes
25   me, so that's why he was walking that way. He sure needs
26   a lesson or two on getting a girl, if that's the truth. You
27   couldn't pay me enough money to go out with that creep.

28   I have to admit, though, sometimes girls are just as bad
29   as guys when it comes to harassing each other. I've seen
30   girls go up to a guy and say things about his "buns" and

1   "pecs," and tell him how much they want to be with him.
2   That's disgusting. I know human beings are a type of
3   animal, but do we really have to act like animals?
4   Whatever happened to mutual respect and admiration
5   for each other? Sure, there's times I look at a guy and
6   think, wow, *he is hot!* But I don't say it to his face.
7   There are other, more subtle ways to get a guy's
8   attention, and a girl's attention. One of the greatest
9   turn-offs is when guys "ogle" you. Would someone
10   please tell them this?
11   If guys would only figure out that most girls are
12   more interested in the things they do for us — like
13   treating us with respect and love — than checking out
14   our bodies, they might have more luck with the girls
15   they want to go out with.
16   Oh yeah, one more thing, do all of you realize that
17   harassment is against the law and you can be criminally
18   charged for doing this? Think about that the next time
19   you start to say something offensive to another person.

What's Your Opinion?

Some people who make harassing statements to others defend themselves by saying they are only paying a compliment to that person. In your opinion, when does a person cross over that fine line of paying a compliment to making a suggestive comment?

Share a few examples of comments you feel are acceptable when seeing a person you are attracted to.

Bullying or making fun of others are other types of harassment. Oftentimes onlookers ignore this because they don't want to be included in the harassment. When you see this going on, what types of action could you take to help the person who is being harassed?

I Won't Experiment on Animals!

1   I don't care what my biology teacher says, I won't
2 dissect animals! I don't care if it's a little bitty worm. God
3 didn't place animals here on this earth for us to cut them
4 apart.

5   I know we can learn a lot of things from cutting open
6 bugs and animals, but it's still wrong. Surely, there has to
7 be some kind of x-ray machine that could teach us the
8 same things.

9   Does my teacher think I want to be a doctor or
10 something? Well, I don't, so I think I should be allowed to
11 learn all these organs and body parts from a book. I mean,
12 is the inside of a person really just like the insides of a
13 worm, a frog or a cat? Besides the fact that it's gross,
14 there has to be a lot of germs floating around. Why should
15 I subject myself to germs unnecessarily?

16   The worst has to be when the teacher asks us to dissect
17 cats! Can you even believe it? I have three beautiful cats
18 who sleep with me, all cuddled up like a ball, every night.
19 Does he really think I'm going to cut up one of these
20 precious creatures?

21   My teacher says I shouldn't feel so bad, because these
22 cats are raised on a farm just for this reason, to be used in
23 classrooms across our country for experimentation. But
24 what makes those cats' lives any less important than my
25 three cats' lives?

26   Just last week in class my teacher showed us a cat who
27 was pregnant with little kittens that had already been cut
28 up. I started to cry. I know the kittens didn't even look like
29 kittens yet, but still ... how could anyone do this to a living,
30 breathing animal?

1   Some of my friends tell me I'm acting ridiculous.
2   They said that without animal experimentation we may
3   never find cures for cancer and all types of other
4   illnesses. One of my friends asked me, "If one of your
5   parents was dying of some disease, and a doctor could
6   find a cure for it by using a cat to try out the medicine
7   on, would you still feel this way?"
8   That question did make me stop and think. Of
9   course, I would choose my parents' lives over a cat's
10 life. But, couldn't we leave all this experimenting to
11 those people who want to be doctors? Why does
12 someone like me, who plans to study weather in college,
13 have to do this?
14   I think my teacher should come up with an
15 alternative assignment for me, or I'll come up with one
16 if he doesn't want to be bothered. This dissecting goes
17 against all my beliefs and feelings about animals and the
18 abuse of them. No matter what my teacher says to try
19 and justify these experiments to me, it's still wrong!

What's Your Opinion?

Should students be allowed to forego the dissecting of animals in biology class? Why or why not? What other types of experiments or assignments might they do in place of dissecting which would still teach the objectives of dissection? What types of animal life are used in your school's science curriculum?

How do you feel about animals being used for experimentation for medicines?

What Harm Could It Be?

1   My parents have been working in the evenings a lot
2 lately. I would be so bored if it weren't for the Internet. It's
3 probably one of the best inventions ever created, don't you
4 agree? Lately, I've met some pretty interesting people in
5 the chat rooms on-line.

6   At first I was a little intimidated by the people I talked
7 to, but after awhile, these people became my friends. I can
8 tell them anything, and since I don't really know them and
9 they don't know me, it doesn't matter what secrets they
10 know.

11   I may have a little problem, though. You see, this one
12 guy and I have gotten really close. He confides to me about
13 all the problems he's having with his girlfriend. I gave him
14 some advice from a girl's point of view.

15   But last night when we were on-line, he told me he and
16 this girl are over. He said that he now knows she wasn't
17 the right person for him. And guess what made him realize
18 this? Me! He said he's never been able to talk with anybody
19 else so openly, and that he really wants to meet me.

20   I know, I know, you're not supposed to give out any
21 personal information to anyone when you're on-line. But I
22 really think this guy is "legit." He's told me all about
23 himself. He works for a computer company, and he's six
24 years older than me. I used to think that was a big age
25 difference, but not anymore.

26   Ron, that's the guy I'm talking about, says that by our
27 age, age really doesn't matter. I'm eighteen and he's
28 twenty-four. He lives three states away from me, but he's
29 even willing to take a trip just to meet me.

30   I haven't given him any information about where I live,

1   yet. But I'm seriously considering it. It's just that Ron
2   seems so much more mature than any of the guys I'm in
3   school with. I'd hate to pass up an opportunity to meet
4   him. Who knows? He might be the guy for me.

5   Of course, I couldn't tell my parents if I decide to
6   meet Ron. They would be so upset with me. That's one
7   of the first things they stressed when we got the Internet
8   at our house, not to get involved with people on-line,
9   and to never, ever give out my real name and address.

10   That rule never bothered me until now. Ron seems
11   so perfect for me. What harm could it be to meet with
12   him just once?

What's Your Opinion?

Tell why, or why not, this person should meet with their new on-line friend.

What are necessary precautions you should take when in a chat room on-line? Have you ever experienced someone who made you suspicious while in a chat room? Explain.

When do you feel it's OK to pursue a relationship which begins on the Internet?

Home Sweet Home

1   It wasn't that long ago I was just like every other
2 normal kid at school. My mom and dad both worked, we
3 had a nice house in a clean neighborhood, and everyone
4 was happy. We even had a Cocker Spaniel named Pup.

5   Then one day Mom and Dad came home from work
6 early. Mom was crying and Dad just kept saying everything
7 was going to be all right. You see, Mom and Dad both
8 worked at this manufacturing plant in town. The plant shut
9 down without giving any notice to its employees, and both
10 my parents lost their jobs.

11   We used to think the plant was such a great place.
12 Nearly everyone in town worked there. Then, another
13 company bought the plant, and things have gone downhill
14 ever since.

15   First, they started by making all the employees take
16 wage cuts. Then, they took away their insurance coverage.
17 Oh, they let them buy insurance at a group rate, which is
18 cheaper, but now my parents not only took wage cuts, but
19 they had a new bill to pay.

20   Six months ago they started cutting peoples' hours
21 back, and now they've shut the plant down completely. My
22 parents said they can't pay the bills anymore. They asked
23 me if I would mind getting a job to help them. None of us
24 are really qualified to do anything. I guess we could take a
25 family outing down to the local fast food restaurant and
26 see if they'll hire all of us. Wouldn't that be fun? *(Said*
27 *sarcastically)*

28   Our house was sold last week. We're living in my aunt
29 and uncle's old camper which is parked in their backyard.
30 My parents made me give Pup to a friend. It's supposed to

1   be a temporary thing, just until we get our feet back on
2   the ground. But it's still not fair.
3   I can't believe we're homeless! That's a word I've
4   heard on TV shows or the news, but I never thought my
5   family would be placed in that category. Wait until all
6   the kids at school hear I'm living in a camper.
7   Unbelievable.
8   I feel bad for my parents, but even more so I am
9   determined to get us out of that camper. It's so
10   humiliating!
11   It seems like there should be somewhere for us to go
12   for help, but my parents are very proud people. They
13   say that's what families are for, to take care of each
14   other, that we would do the same for anyone else in our
15   family. I say, who wants to be homeless? Forget all that
16   pride and get whatever help is available to us. Who
17   knows, maybe there's even money available to us that
18   would let my parents go back for some schooling, so
19   they could get a half decent job.
20   I really don't know what to do. I'm so frustrated and
21   tired of living in an area three feet by three feet! OK,
22   not really ... but it seems that small.
23   I guess I better start filling out job applications.

What's Your Opinion?

What steps do you think this person's family should take?

Are there ways you can think to help a person who's homeless? Explain.

Try to imagine how you would feel if your family suddenly found themselves at the mercy of others, no jobs, no home ... how might this experience change you?

Head of the Class

1   All my life I've wanted to graduate at the top of my
2 class. I don't know why it's that important to me, but it is.
3 I guess part of the reason is because my mom was so close
4 to graduating number one in her class, but during the last
5 nine weeks of school another student beat her out. She
6 doesn't offer any excuses for it, she says she was beat fair
7 and square. But I think she's always been a little
8 disappointed in herself because of it. She never says so,
9 it's just the way she looks when she talks about it.

10   She will be so proud of me if I do this. Up until this
11 year, I had the number one spot wrapped up. No one was
12 even close to me. I've spent hours in the library studying
13 in order to do well. No one handed me my good grades, it
14 takes a lot of work. That's why I'm so upset that I may
15 graduate number two.

16   I hate to sound like I'm some immature kid whining,
17 but I really don't think what's happened this year is fair.
18 You see, this kid, Hans, came to our school this year as a
19 foreign exchange student from Germany. I give him credit,
20 he's brilliant. He's challenged me to do my best in every
21 class. I finally met someone who cared as much about his
22 studies as me.

23   The thing is, now that it's time to graduate, he's
24 actually ahead of me. I have over a 4.0, but his GPA is like
25 .0001 higher than mine. Can you believe it? I guess I didn't
26 realize that foreign exchange students were even in the
27 running for holding a class rank. I don't know, shouldn't
28 they receive some kind of honorary diplomas or
29 something? It's not like Hans is staying in the country, he's
30 leaving as soon as school is out.

1   I never dreamed I would have to give up my
2   valedictorian spot to him. I think he was as surprised as
3   I was when the teachers came to us and told us what
4   was going on. I guess their opinions are divided on this
5   subject, too.
6   Some people don't realize that there are special
7   scholarships offered to students who graduate number
8   one in their class. It doesn't seem right that this should
9   be taken from me, when Hans isn't even going to college
10 in the States.
11   I guess the whole matter is going before the school
12 board on Monday night. I never knew my academic
13 success was going to cause such a debate in the town.
14 Everyone seems to have an opinion about this.
15   I wish everyone would just let Hans and I work
16 something out. I think we really could come up with a
17 plan we'd both be happy about. But will anyone listen to
18 us? No. I guess I'm just supposed to sit back and wait
19 for the verdict.
20   Oh well, no matter what the decisions is, I'm glad
21 Hans came to America. He's been a good friend.

What's Your Opinion?

How do you feel this situation should be handled? Do you
feel this should be handled any differently than if a new student
moved into the district and took over the number one class rank?
Explain.

Does your school have a policy regarding foreign exchange
students and their ability to hold class rank? If you're not sure,
perhaps this topic should be addressed. This situation could
happen to you. If it did, how would you feel?

New Driving Laws

1   It is going to be a loooong six months until I get my
2 driver's license. You see, our state passed a new law that
3 says every sixteen-year-old has to wait until they've had
4 their permit six months before they can take their driver's
5 test. It is such an unfair law!

6   Do you realize that in some states fifteen-year-olds can
7 drive? So what's up with our state legislature? Oh, they
8 justify these changes by saying that statistics show sixteen-
9 year-olds have the highest number of accidents on the
10 highways. They think these new laws will decrease these
11 numbers.

12   I think that is really stupid. I mean, the same kids who
13 are getting into these accidents when they are sixteen are
14 going to be the same kids who get in accidents at sixteen
15 and a half. Why penalize all of us because of a few?

16   My mom and dad think the new laws are great. Not
17 only do I have to wait until I'm sixteen and a half to take
18 my test, but I have to have fifty supervised hours of
19 instruction with an adult, defined as someone twenty-one
20 or older. So now, my seventeen-year-old friends who have
21 their licenses can't even take me driving!

22   Here's the worst part of it all. Once I get my license, I
23 have to be in by eleven o'clock! It used to be midnight.
24 Now I have to wait until I'm seventeen and a half to stay
25 out until midnight. How am I supposed to go to a late show
26 and make it home on time? My parents say, "Just go to an
27 earlier movie." I tell them, "Thanks for the advice."

28   The only people who understand how I feel are other
29 sixteen-year-olds who fall under these laws. I've been
30 driving with my permit for three months now, and I know

1 I could pass my test. It's making me crazy that I have to
2 wait three more months. The entire summer will be over
3 before I get my license!
4   Personally, I don't think these laws are going to
5 make a bit of difference. Maybe they just need to make
6 the test a little harder in order to pass. Then some of
7 the people who are passing their tests wouldn't pass. I
8 just don't think it's fair that all sixteen-year-olds have to
9 pay the price for those who have driven irresponsibly in
10 the past.
11   *(Pause)* **Maybe the extra driving experience will help.**
12 **I guess only time will tell.**

What's Your Opinion?

How do you feel about this actor's state driving laws, i.e., age requirement, supervised driving instruction and curfew?

Write your own ideas as to what you believe are fair regulations regarding new drivers.

Why Am I Here?

1   You know, there's lots of different types of abuse. We
2 hear everyday about physical abuse, someone beats their
3 kids, or someone's boyfriend is beating them up. But what
4 about the abuse called neglect?

5   From the time I was a little boy I wondered why I was
6 even born. I can't remember either one of my parents ever
7 acting as though they loved me. At first, I didn't know any
8 better. I thought it was normal to make your own
9 breakfast, iron your own clothes, and tuck yourself in at
10 night. I was only five years old when I was doing all of
11 these things. I might have been even younger than that
12 when I started taking care of myself, but that's the earliest
13 I can remember.

14   My parents don't ever hit me. In fact, I don't remember
15 them even yelling at me much. I've always been able to do
16 pretty much what I want, as long as I'm not bothering
17 them. I used to think it was pretty cool. I would get up, get
18 something to eat, then take off on my bike. I'd be gone the
19 whole day, until it was dark outside. There was always
20 food in the fridge when I got home, but no one ever cared
21 what I was doing.

22   Last year I made a good friend named Bennie. He
23 asked me to spend the night at his house. The time I spent
24 with Bennie's family was the first time I began to
25 understand that my life wasn't the way other kids lived. His
26 mom cooked supper and everyone sat around the table
27 laughing and talking. That night they made us go to bed by
28 midnight. His mom actually gave Bennie a kiss and told
29 him she loved him before we went to bed. Bennie was a
30 little embarrassed, but he has no idea how much I wished

1 it was me instead of him being told I was loved.
2   It felt really good to be with a family who cared
3 about each other. I mean, sometimes the other kids at
4 school tell me I don't know how lucky I have it. I'm
5 always allowed to do whatever I want and go wherever
6 I want, as long as I find my own rides, of course. But the
7 fact is, I wish just once my parents would ask me where
8 I'm going to be, or how I'm getting home.
9   It's like I just exist, with no meaning, and no love. I
10 never realized how unhappy I am. I wish there was some
11 way I could reach out to my parents and tell them how
12 I feel. They'd probably just look at me funny and ask me
13 what I've been smoking. It's no use. I guess that's just
14 the way my life is supposed to be.

What's Your Opinion?

If this person was your friend, what advice would you give him to make his life happier?

When a child is provided with food and shelter, but no love, do you feel this is a form of abuse which should be dealt with by a community service provider, the same type of place which provides help in cases of physical abuse? Explain.

Racism Is, Sadly, Alive and Well

1 It's so hard to believe that in this day and age, there is
2 still so much prejudice around. No matter who you talk to
3 it seems as though there's at least one group of people
4 who they have problems with for one reason or another.

5 Let's see, it might be the color of a person's skin, or
6 the way their eyes slant too much, or too little, or it could
7 be the church a person goes to, the God they believe in,
8 the way a person talks, how much money their family
9 makes, where a person lives, or where their ancestors
10 came from. You name it, everyone's got some kind of
11 hang-up.

12 I've heard that Italians have bad tempers, Scots are
13 tight with their money, Jews are all rich, African-
14 Americans are all poor, and the Irish are all too loud and
15 obnoxious. I could go on and on about all the things I've
16 heard from other people.

17 I wouldn't have any friends if I were to listen to the
18 prejudices of others. How does this happen to us? None of
19 us are born feeling this way towards others. We're taught
20 to be this way.

21 Children are so loving and will play with anyone when
22 they're toddlers. One of my earliest memories is when my
23 mother took me to McDonald's Playland. I'm caucasian
24 and there was a little African-American girl there. Right
25 away we started playing together. I noticed her skin was a
26 different color than mine, but I thought it was fascinating.
27 She had a glow about her and her hair was in all these tiny
28 little braids that were so cool.

29 It wasn't until an older boy came up to us and said,
30 "Don't you two know that black kids don't play with white

1   kids?" that I thought maybe I was doing something
2   wrong.
3   I ran over to my mother crying. When she heard why
4   I was upset she marched me right back to the little dark-
5   skinned child and reminded me how much fun we were
6   having. She said to keep playing together until it was
7   time to go. She also said very loudly, so the other boy
8   and his parents could hear, "My children may play with
9   any other children who are kind and fun to play with. I
10 want you to remember that."
11   I always have remembered my mother's words. I'm
12 just so sorry that other parents don't tell their children
13 the same thing.
14   Getting rid of racism would be so easy if all of us
15 would make the commitment to see each other for who
16 we are and not for what we look like. Can you imagine
17 a world where people get to know each other before
18 they decide whether or not they want to continue a
19 relationship with a person? So many good friendships
20 never happen because we look at a person and decide
21 their nose is too big, or they're too fat.
22   I am so thankful I was raised to give all people a
23 chance. If you weren't taught to believe the way I do
24 about others, please think about what I've said and
25 make some changes in your attitudes, if changes are
26 needed. I promise you, you will meet some wonderfully
27 interesting people by doing this, and you'll make some
28 lifetime friendships you may have missed out on
29 otherwise.

What's Your Opinion?

Do you share the opinion of this actor, that racism is alive and well? Explain. If you've seen examples of racism, share these.

Tell what steps you can take to help our world eliminate racism.

A Patriotic Tribute

1   Ever since I was a little girl I get all sentimental
2 whenever I see our flag waving in the sky. I guess I'm lucky
3 my parents brought me up to understand the symbolism
4 this piece of cloth represents.

5   Lots of my ancestors fought in the wars that defended
6 our freedoms. Many of my relatives died on foreign soil, so
7 that I can enjoy being free today.

8   My grandparents and my parents never let me take our
9 freedom for granted. Every Memorial Day our family
10 attends the parade in town. A few of my great-uncles
11 march with their friends, wearing their old uniforms. They
12 stand as straight and proud on that day as if they were still
13 young men marching off to war.

14   I get the chills when I see all these gray-haired men go
15 by. They are so proud of who they are and the country for
16 which they fought. We always salute my uncles as they
17 march by, and when they see us, tears stream down their
18 faces. I sometimes wonder if they're thinking about all the
19 friends they saw killed right before their eyes.

20   Once on the fourth of July, our town held a gathering
21 by this beautiful lake. There was a brass band playing all
22 the songs from each branch of the service. They asked all
23 the men and women veterans and those presently serving
24 in the armed forces to stand as they heard their own song.

25   The band would play the Navy song, then the Marines,
26 and so on. As I looked over the crowd and saw these
27 people standing so proudly when they heard their military
28 song played I just broke down and cried. Some of the men
29 wore their full uniforms, even in the heat of a July
30 afternoon. Some were in wheelchairs, and stood feebly,

1 shaking all the way up, holding tightly onto their
2 younger family member next to them for support.
3   It's hard for me to talk about it without crying. Tears
4 of pride, of course. We are so fortunate to live in the
5 United States of America. But what makes me cry even
6 more, because of sadness this time, is when I see kids
7 my age making fun of some of these older veterans, or
8 laughing during the National Anthem, or burning flags
9 just for kicks. I want to shake them and scream, "What
10 is wrong with all of you?" I'd like to gather all of them
11 up and ship them off to live in some third world nations
12 for awhile. Maybe that would make them appreciate the
13 lives they have here in America.
14   I like what one honored veteran said. He asked all of
15 us, the next time we watch fireworks on the fourth of
16 July, to remember that many Americans heard the same
17 loud booms and whistles we will enjoy, but that they
18 heard those sounds as enemy artillery was being fired at
19 them. That analogy gives all of us something to think
20 about, doesn't it?

What's Your Opinion?

Write your ideas on what it means to be an American. Share
your opinion on whether you would be willing to fight in a war
to preserve this country's freedom. If you could thank all the
soldiers who lost their lives to allow you a life of freedom, what
are some things you might say to them?

Free to Dream

1   Sometimes people tell me I'm nothing but a dreamer.
2 Part of what they say is true. I am a dreamer, but ... there's
3 something about me that makes me different from just any
4 dreamer. I'm also a doer.

5   When we're small children, everyone tells us we can do
6 anything we set our minds to, and we can realize our
7 dreams. Those words sound wonderful, and they are ...
8 somewhat true. The part that's often left out is the fact
9 that realizing our dreams takes lots and lots of hard work
10 and determination. And the only people who succeed are
11 the ones who never give up.

12   I used to just sit around and dream about becoming
13 this famous successful writer one day. The problem was, I
14 found myself sitting around all the time thinking about how
15 great it was going to be when I was famous and successful.
16 Meanwhile, no one was reading anything I was writing. It
17 just stayed in my computer or my journal for me to read.
18 How was I going to succeed in writing that way?

19   I'm thankful I had a teacher who really encouraged me
20 to pursue my dream. She showed me how to become
21 involved in writing. Now I'm writing articles for our school
22 newspaper. In the summer I'm going to serve as an intern
23 at the newspaper in town.

24   I've also signed up for some classes at the local college.
25 My goal is to submit some of my stories for publication.
26 Even if nothing is accepted, at least I feel as though I'm
27 taking steps toward achieving my goal. And no matter how
28 many rejection slips I might get from publishing houses, I'll
29 keep trying. There has to be somebody out there who likes
30 what I write.

1   All I know is that dreams are only realized by taking
2   one tiny step at a time. And while I know it may be years
3   before I reach my goal, at least I feel I'm doing
4   something about getting there besides sitting on my
5   rear end dreaming about it.
6   If I never achieve success as a writer, I will have
7   achieved success as a person, because I would rather try
8   and fail, than never try at all.

What's Your Opinion?

Share what your dream is, what you hope to achieve in your future. Then tell what steps you're taking in order to see that dream become a reality.

Is No One Allowed to Date Anymore?

1   Guys have me totally confused! They are so possessive!
2 As soon as you start to talk to a guy he thinks he owns you.
3 All of a sudden you're not allowed to call anyone else, ride
4 in a car with anyone else or smile at another guy.
5   Just what does the word "date" mean, anyway? No one
6 my age uses the word anymore. I guess our generation has
7 its own vocabulary. According to my mother, dating is
8 when you really like one guy, but there's no commitment,
9 so it's still OK to go out with another guy if someone asks
10 you. I thought that's what "talking to someone" meant for
11 my generation. But, it hasn't been working that way for
12 me.
13   Take this guy I've been "talking" to. We decided we
14 wanted to see each other, but not be considered a couple,
15 or "going out" together. That was cool with me. I have lots
16 of guy friends I like to do things with, so the idea of being
17 with one guy exclusively is nothing I'm interested in.
18   Sure enough, as soon as this guy heard I had talked to
19 another guy at work, he started flipping out on me. I was
20 like, "OK, are you and me suddenly a couple?" Of course,
21 he said, "No, but that doesn't mean you're supposed to be
22 talking to other guys."
23   So I asked him, "Do you want to be going out with
24 me?"
25   He said, "No, I don't have time to be tied down to a
26 girl. I just thought when I did want to take a girl out, you
27 wanted to go out with me. Was I wrong?"
28   I had to laugh in his face. Did he expect me to just sit

1 around waiting for him to suddenly have a whim to take
2 a girl out, and oh, lucky me, he would call me to fulfill
3 his need for a girl that night? Give me a break! Is this
4 some new kind of caveman attitude that says a woman
5 becomes a possession as soon as a guy takes her to a
6 movie?

7   Needless to say, this guy is history. Like I already
8 said, I have lots of guy friends to have fun with. Maybe
9 one day I'll be lucky enough to meet someone who just
10 wants to "date," as my mom calls it, without getting so
11 possessive. If you know a guy like that, give him my
12 phone number, OK?

What's Your Opinion?

What are your opinions on "dating" or "talking to
someone"? Is it OK to go out with several girls or guys at one
time? For example, is it OK to go out with one person to the
movies on Friday night, and go out with a different person on
Saturday night? Or is it better to "date" one person at a time?
Share some of your ideas about "dating."

Can You Be Friends after Dating?

1   My old girlfriend is making me crazy. We went out for
2 almost a year, then things just started falling apart. I don't
3 know, maybe we started taking each other for granted or
4 something, but we started fighting over everything.

5   I'm still trying to figure out how something so good
6 turned bad. We tried working on our relationship. We
7 started to go out more with our friends, thinking that
8 maybe we were just together too much. That helped, but
9 still things were different.

10   We both decided that it would be better if we broke up.
11 She wanted to still be friends, and so did I. But I'm having
12 a really hard time dealing with this new "friendship." How
13 do you go back to being just friends with someone you
14 really cared about? I'm so used to having her around. I see
15 her and I want to be able to put my arm around her and
16 tell her I still love her, that I know we can work things out.

17   Last week she called me on my birthday. That was
18 sweet of her, I guess, but it just made me start to think that
19 maybe she still cared about me ... as more than a friend. I
20 let all these crazy thoughts go through my head, like
21 maybe we could get back together. And maybe she wanted
22 to get together, too, but was too shy to say anything.

23   So, the next time I saw her out, I asked her if she felt
24 the same way. She asked me where I got that idea, that she
25 was just being a good friend, wishing me a happy birthday.
26 She said she's really happy just being friends and that I
27 need to move on with my life. Is there anyone out there
28 who can tell me how to do that?

1　My friends tell me that what I need is a new girl. I
2　say, why would I want another girl? It's a girl who has
3　me so mixed up and confused to begin with.
4　　The thing is, I can't imagine going on with my life
5　and her not being a part of it. If all we can be is friends,
6　I guess I need to accept that. Maybe after some time has
7　passed we can be friends, but right now it still hurts too
8　much. The question is, what do I do with myself
9　between now and then? It feels like the hurt will never
10　go away.
11　　When I try to talk to her as a friend, I leave feeling
12　depressed. I'm mad at myself for blowing a good thing,
13　and I don't know if I'll ever get another chance with her.
14　Should I even want another chance with her? She is
15　obviously over me.
16　　I don't know what to do.

What's Your Opinion?

Is it possible to be friends with an ex-boyfriend or girlfriend?
What could this person do to make the adjustment from a dating
relationship to a friendship easier?

If you've ever been in this position, share how you handled
this situation.

Do Something Worthwhile with Your Life!

1   Last year I was such a nobody. I mean it. I didn't even
2 realize how I was wasting my life away. I thought it was
3 great spending my summer vacation sleeping in until noon
4 every day, waking up just in time to eat lunch. Then I'd
5 catch up on my favorite soap operas and talk shows until
6 supper. At night I'd cruise the diamond downtown with my
7 friends to see how many cute guys I could meet.

8   Luckily, I got a great teacher this year who made a big
9 difference in my life. In class we studied all the different
10 cultures which make up our country. I guess Mr. Jenkins
11 opened my eyes, so to speak, to the world around me.

12   Let's face it, my world truly did revolve around only
13 me. I was always so worried about my hair, my makeup
14 and the latest fashions everyone was wearing. It was a
15 great life and I had lots of fun, but I really wasn't making
16 any difference to anyone. No one benefited from my
17 existence.

18   Mr. Jenkins helped all of us to understand how we have
19 to get involved in our world. There are so many ways we
20 can help other people, so many small things we can do in
21 order to make our world a better place.

22   One of the first things our class decided to sponsor was
23 a school blood drive. Last year I would have flatly refused
24 to participate. But now I understand that in just one short
25 hour, I'm able to give of myself and maybe save someone
26 else's life.

27   At Thanksgiving time, we held a dance where each
28 person had to donate one item of boxed or canned food in

1   order to get into the dance. You wouldn't believe how
2   much food we were able to collect. And everyone had a
3   great time at the dance, too.

4   When Christmas came along we held a contest for
5   the different grades in our school. It was a "Bundle Up"
6   project collecting warm clothing for needy people in our
7   community. In the school lobby we had a mannequin for
8   each grade level. They were each dressed in school
9   clothes, and the object was to bundle the mannequin up
10 in winter clothing.

11   For every twenty articles of clothing brought in to
12 the school for a certain grade level, we would put a
13 piece of winter clothing on their mannequin, like a hat,
14 scarf or mittens. The first grade level to dress their
15 mannequin for cold weather received free tickets for the
16 basketball game and the aftergame dance.

17   For our final nine weeks' grade, Mr. Jenkins let us
18 form groups, and we all had to create our own project
19 to help our school or community. My friends and I
20 decided to use everything we know about fashion and
21 makeup and try to help others with our knowledge.

22   We gathered all of our old makeup and any clothes
23 we didn't want anymore. We headed for the local
24 women's shelter for abused women and children. The
25 people in charge gladly let us offer free makeovers to
26 any of the women who wished to have one.

27   I can't put into words the feelings I felt after seeing
28 these women smile when they saw themselves fixed up
29 a little bit. They were so used to being put down and
30 battered, that to look in the mirror and see their pretty
31 faces made them light up.

32   I'm not trying to stand up here and preach to all of
33 you about how you should be living your lives. I only
34 want you to know that life can be about so much more
35 than all the typical things teens are interested in. I had

1 no idea life could hold so much meaning for me.
2   Don't lose out on a single day. Take the time for
3 others, and believe me, you will be so much happier. The
4 saying is true, it's much better to give than to receive.

What's Your Opinion?

Share community projects you and your friends are involved with. List some new ideas you may be able to start this year.

In what ways do you think becoming involved with your community can change a person?

College-Bound? Or Not?

1 My senior year ... I finally made it! High school has
2 been great. To tell you the truth, I'd be happy just staying
3 here. Everyone else keeps going on and on about what
4 college they plan to attend, but not me.

5 And I don't care what Mom and Dad say, I don't want
6 to go to college. You don't understand how hard this is for
7 me to tell my parents. Ever since I can remember my mom
8 led me to believe a person *had* to go to college. She would
9 tell me that after elementary school came junior high
10 school, then high school, then college.

11 It wasn't until junior high that my friends told me
12 college was something you *chose* to do. At first I got mad
13 at them and told them they didn't know what they were
14 talking about. Then I got mad at my mom, because I
15 realized she was lying to me all those years.

16 Mom says she didn't purposely lie ... she just figured
17 that by the time I knew the truth I would want to go to
18 college, so it wouldn't really matter. According to Mom she
19 told me this for my own good. She doesn't want to see me
20 choose not to go to college, wind up in some minimum-
21 wage-paying job and decide when I'm thirty to go to
22 college then.

23 That's what Mom did. She says I'll never understand
24 how difficult it was to go to college full-time while working
25 full-time and having a baby to take care of. She thought
26 she might have a nervous breakdown, but ... she did it.
27 And I'm proud of her for that, but why does she think it's
28 so important to go to college?

29 I have my own plans. I'm going to go to a really good
30 beauty school. Within five years I plan to have my own

1 shop with a few people working for me. After ten years
2 my shop should be making enough money that I won't
3 have to work. I'll just run the business end of things
4 from home and let my employees deal with the people.
5   See, Mom and Dad don't realize that I've got plans
6 of my own. When I set my mind to something I usually
7 succeed. I just wish my parents would give me the
8 chance to prove to them I can do this. I know I'm good
9 at doing hair and nails. I don't care how many people
10 tell me I'm too smart for beauty school, I know that a
11 career in cosmetology is worthwhile. Look how good
12 you make people feel when you give them a great new
13 look. The question is, how do I convince my parents that
14 I'm right? Mom already said my parents will pay my way
15 through college, but not beauty school. What am I
16 supposed to do?

What's Your Opinion?

What options do you feel this teen has? If your parents were deadset on you going to college and you didn't want to go, share what you would say to persuade your parents to allow you to follow your own dreams.

Get Educated!

1   I've been working at a local department store for the
2 past year. Let me tell you, if anything convinced me to go
3 to college, this job is it.

4   All my friends tell me I'm lucky. They think I have it
5 made just because I'm not flipping burgers somewhere like
6 them, and I don't go home smelling like fried food.

7   But I do go home with a sore neck and a backache. You
8 wouldn't believe the people who come through my
9 checkout line. These big strong men will throw a twenty-
10 pound bag of dog food onto the counter, then stand there
11 and watch me while I struggle to put the bag into the buggy
12 after I scan it.

13   We have to work at least four hours before we get a
14 break. Have you ever tried standing with your head tilted
15 down toward a cash register for four hours? Talk about a
16 stiff neck! I've started taking an Advil before I even go to
17 work.

18   Of course ... there are the store managers. They're not
19 all bad, but for the most part, they treat us cashiers like
20 we're idiots.

21   We've all been told a thousand times to straighten the
22 items in our aisle when we're not busy with a customer.
23 The other night was a slow night, so I straightened all
24 those little packs of gum and lifesavers, et cetera, et
25 cetera.

26   When the manager came by she said, "Let's go, you
27 know you're supposed to be straightening items when
28 you're not busy."

29   I wanted to scream back, "How many times can you
30 straighten a pack of gum. How straight can it get? It's a

1 rectangle! I've already put the rectangle straight up and
2 down, what more should I do?!"
3   But, of course, I just smiled and messed up my nice
4 neat candy rows so that I could straighten them one
5 more time.
6   Oh yeah, one more thing. These places always
7 advertise flexible hours. Huh! That's one of the biggest
8 lies I've ever heard. They ask you when you're available
9 to work. You tell them, "I'm available on Saturday
10 morning and afternoon, and Tuesday and Thursday
11 nights."
12   So, when do they schedule you? Saturday night, and
13 Monday and Wednesday evenings! How hard is it to get
14 that straight?
15   I don't complain a lot, but hey, if you ask me how I
16 like my job, I'm going to be honest. It stinks! I can't wait
17 to start college and have a real job someday. I have no
18 idea what my job will be, but there's one thing I do
19 know. When I'm working I want to go home at the end
20 of the day feeling appreciated, and also feeling proud of
21 what I do. That's just not happening now.
22   I'm counting down. Only two hundred thirty-two
23 days until I go to college.

What's Your Opinion?

How do you feel about this teen's complaints? Does she/he have a right to be upset or does she/he just have an attitude? If you work, do you feel mistreated by your boss at times? Explain.

Share what kind of jobs you feel are the best for high school students to have.

Making a Big Mistake

1   Man, did I mess up. And it looks like I'm going to be
2 paying for it a long time. You see, I thought I had a group
3 of really good friends. We've been hanging out together
4 since seventh grade. We've always acted a little crazy when
5 we were together, but last summer we did something really
6 stupid.

7   Let's see ... where should I begin? I guess I'll start with
8 the night we started the phone calls.

9   You see, there's this teacher at our school who's a real
10 jerk. It's not just me who thinks that. Probably if you
11 surveyed the other teachers they'd even agree. He puts all
12 the students down and reminds us every day how stupid we
13 are.

14   Well, one night when we were bored us guys decided to
15 call this teacher on the phone. I guess we got a little
16 carried away. We called him a few choice names I'm not
17 very proud of. At the time, it was pretty funny, actually. In
18 fact, it was so funny we called him again ... and then
19 another night ... and another night. Before we knew it,
20 calling up our teacher became a weekly ritual. It felt good
21 to be able to tell him exactly how we felt about him, and
22 he didn't know who was saying it.

23   Now's when you can call us stupid, and I'll agree. I
24 guess our teacher had called the police after about the first
25 three phone calls we made. The police traced the phone
26 line and found out it was me making the calls. My teacher
27 pressed harassment charges against me.

28   That's not even the worst of it. When the police came
29 to my house to question me, my mom had an attorney
30 there. He told me I'd better tell all the names of everyone

1 involved, because if I didn't talk now, and more facts
2 came out in court, I could be in even worse trouble.

3   What was I supposed to do? You're right, I was a
4 coward. The guy scared me half to death. So, I told. I
5 gave the policemen all my friends' names. I didn't tell
6 just so they would be in trouble, too. I was scared. I
7 wanted to do everything the lawyer told me to do, so that
8 the rest of my life wouldn't be completely messed up.

9   Now I have to go to court before a judge and tell
10 everything one more time. My attorney says I'll probably
11 get probation since this is the first time I've been in
12 trouble. Man, I really messed up. Not only did I get in
13 trouble with the law and my family, I no longer have any
14 friends. They're all so mad at me for giving the cops
15 their names that I have been unanimously voted out of
16 the group. I'm lucky if even one person at school speaks
17 to me all day long.

18   What a life. I don't know what to do to make things
19 better.

What's Your Opinion?

How do you think you would have handled things if it was you in this situation? What's your opinion on how this teen handled things? Is it right, or wrong, to tell on your friends when "your back is put up against the wall," so to speak?

Baby-sitting

1   I thought I was going to love baby-sitting. I couldn't
2 wait until I was old enough. I've always loved little kids.
3 Getting paid to watch the kids was like a dream job for me.
4 Little did I realize how unfairly baby sitters are treated.

5   Like just a week ago I was supposed to baby-sit three
6 evenings after school. I was counting on those jobs
7 because I'm trying to save up enough money to put a down
8 payment on a used car.

9   Well, on two of the three nights, just five minutes
10 before I was supposed to leave, the mother called me and
11 told me that she and her husband changed their minds
12 about going out. Oops, she said. She forgot to call me.

13   How nice of her. I could've gone to the basketball game
14 with my friends, but no, I thought I had a baby-sitting job.
15 By the time the lady called to cancel, my friends had
16 already left for the game, and I didn't have another ride. I
17 was stuck home by myself and didn't make any money!

18   The next night I got to the people's house at the time
19 they asked me to be there. It was another hour before they
20 left. They were running late or something. That was fine
21 with me until it came time to pay me at the end of the
22 night. They didn't pay me anything for the hour I sat there
23 while they were getting ready.

24   They said, "Well, since we didn't leave until nine
25 o'clock, we thought it was fair to pay you from that time.
26 OK?"

27   What was I supposed to say? I just shook my head and
28 took the money. It will be a long time before I'm free to
29 baby-sit for either of those families again.

30   The third night I baby-sat was the last straw. I mean,

1 these people are really good to me, but it seems like
2 their kids are always sick! When I got to their house, the
3 mother said she was really sorry to tell me, but that the
4 baby had bronchitis and was running a temperature of
5 one hundred degrees. Since it wasn't too high, they
6 were going ahead with their plans. She left a number
7 where I could call her if I needed her.

8   That was one of the longest nights of my life. The
9 baby screamed for over an hour straight. Then she
10 started coughing and making this sound when she
11 breathed. I got really scared, so I called her parents at
12 their party. They were home within the next half hour.
13 They paid me for the whole night even though I was only
14 there two hours.

15   You might think, then what are you complaining
16 about? I'm complaining because I ended up with
17 bronchitis and missed five days of school! Shouldn't
18 parents tell you if their child is sick *before* you get
19 there? Give us a choice as to whether we even want to
20 baby-sit a child who's sick. I was so far behind in school
21 after getting sick, that I couldn't take any jobs for two
22 weeks.

23   I know I'd much rather make money by watching
24 children, but I'm seriously considering getting a job at
25 Kmart or something. I know I won't like it, but at least
26 it's dependable and I'll know how much money I'm
27 making every week.

28   I just wish parents were a little more considerate of
29 us baby sitters. Maybe after hearing my side of the
30 story, parents will understand why they have such a
31 hard time getting high school students to baby-sit!

What's Your Opinion?

Share some of your experiences baby-sitting, good and bad.

What do you feel is a fair wage for baby-sitting? Should high-school students state a certain wage or simply accept whatever the parents offer?

What suggestions could you give this teen about improving her frustrating baby-sitting experiences?

Politics Anyone? Doubtful!

1   I've always been fascinated by politics and the
2 government. Ever since I was a little child tagging along
3 with my grandfather to city council meetings, I thought I
4 would go into public service.

5   But I'm starting to change my mind. Every time I open
6 the newspaper I read about another politician who's been
7 arrested for fraud or tax evasion or who knows what else?

8   My mom says that's just politics. She thinks a lot of
9 good people go into politics, but that once you're in there,
10 you learn how tough the job is.

11   I'm not sure it's possible to stay honest. In order to get
12 funding for your district you have to "play games." It's
13 kind of like an "I'll vote for your bill if you vote for mine"
14 game.

15   And how about all these officials they're finding with
16 ties to the mob? I think that's terrible, but what would you
17 do if you were mayor and the mob came and threatened
18 that if you didn't cooperate with them, your family
19 wouldn't be safe? I don't know ...

20   When I look at the morality of some of our past and
21 present leaders it makes me wonder about where our
22 country is headed. It's almost as if everything is tolerated
23 anymore. There's all kinds of issues like abortion, gay
24 rights, school vouchers, gun control, you name it.

25   Things would be so much easier if the world was black
26 and white, but there's so much gray out there I'm not sure
27 what I think is right or wrong anymore.

28   My mom tells me that if I'm truly interested in
29 government I should get involved. There are ways I can be
30 a leader in honest organizations. Right now I'm running for

1 president of student council. Our school has a Future
2 Business Leaders of America Club. I'm joining that, too.
3   I guess I'll try out my skills as a leader in these
4 organizations just to see if I really do enjoy community
5 service. If I like it, I'll take one step at a time. Maybe I'll
6 be one of the few teens who sit on their district's school
7 board. When I get to college I'd like to major in political
8 science. Maybe I'll get a chance to be nominated to
9 serve on the student council at college.
10   I think politics is in my blood. No matter how bleak
11 things seem, someone like me, and others, has to step
12 in and try to run things with honesty and fairness. All I
13 ask is this, if you ever notice me accepting cash bribes
14 under the table, grab my face and yell, *"You're just*
15 *another dirty politican!"* Maybe if you're there to
16 remind me of what's right and wrong I won't get sucked
17 in with all the others.

What's Your Opinion?

Think of a few of the political scandals you've heard and
read about. Share your feelings about whether personal morality
should be an issue as long as the politician is doing a good job
serving the people.

Do you think it's possible for a politician to stay honest once
they're thrown into the political world? Explain.

Pay Your Fair Share

1   When I first got my driver's license I was so excited. I
2   had been saving money for years so that I'd have enough
3   money to put down on a used car. Lucky for me, my aunt
4   and uncle were selling their car, and it was one I could
5   afford.

6   Finally, I'd have more freedom. The days of asking my
7   parents to drive me everywhere I wanted to go were over.
8   If I was bored, I didn't have to sit around being bored, I
9   could just hop in the car and go visit a friend. We could go
10   to the mall, or just drive around and see what was
11   happening.

12   Well, let me tell you, the excitement of those first
13   weeks wore off pretty quick. My parents made me go get
14   a job to help pay the car payment and all of my gas. I'm
15   not really complaining about that, I understand having a
16   car is a great expense. There's no way I could have my own
17   car without helping Mom and Dad pay for it.

18   No ... it's not my mom and dad I started getting
19   annoyed with. It was my best friends! All of a sudden I was
20   the one who had a car, and I was the one who had to drive
21   everywhere. Like I said, at first I didn't mind. But after
22   awhile, when no one was pitching in any money to help pay
23   for gas, I got tired of it.

24   I don't think my friends ever thought about it. It's not
25   like they were trying to take advantage of me, even though
26   that's what I felt like. They just never had to work to pay
27   for their own gas, so they didn't realize what I was dealing
28   with.

29   One week when I was riding around on "E," I begged
30   my mom for some gas money. She gave me five bucks just

1   so I could get to work, but she also told me I needed to
2   speak up and let my friends know that I needed some
3   help paying for gas if I was going to be the chaffeur
4   everytime all of us went out.
5   I told her I couldn't say anything, that my friends
6   would think I was terrible if I asked them for gas money.
7   It would be too embarrassing.
8   Mom said that until I got up the nerve to discuss this
9   with my friends she wasn't helping me out on the gas
10 again. I understand her point of view, because I agree
11 that my friends should help me out. But, I can't ask
12 them for money. I don't know what to do.

What's Your Opinion?

Share how you and your friends handle this same situation when you go out. Think of some ways this teen could solve her problem and write them down.

Are All Illegal Drugs Really Bad for You?

1   First of all, I want you to know that I am completely
2 against the use of illegal drugs. I know that there are
3 hundreds of senseless deaths each year caused by them.
4 People can act just plain crazy when they're high on
5 something.

6   But, there is one issue for which I have mixed
7 emotions, and that's the use of marijuana. Oh, I've read all
8 the arguments against its use. Some reports say that
9 smoking it causes memory loss. I've also read that it dulls
10 your senses. I guess that's not good, especially if you're
11 going to be driving or something.

12   But, I've also read some good things about pot. A lot
13 of people say that it helps those who are in constant pain.
14 For some reason it's reported that smoking marijuana
15 dulls the excruciating pain many live with every day of their
16 lives.

17   There was an article in a magazine I was reading that
18 talked about a woman who had bone cancer. There wasn't
19 a day that went by when she wasn't in horrible pain. She
20 had taken every kind of pain pill her doctor could
21 prescribe, but none of them helped. It got so bad that the
22 woman thought about committing suicide.

23   Then one of her friends told her to try smoking
24 marijuana. They had heard of it helping people who are in
25 pain. The woman was so desperate that she was willing to
26 try anything. She was amazed at how well she felt after
27 smoking the marijuana.

28   Somehow the police learned about what she was doing.

1   They told her she would have to stop or be arrested.

2   Does that seem right? Here's a poor person whose
3   pain was relieved by smoking pot. The woman was
4   finally able to somewhat enjoy what little of her life was
5   left. But the laws prevented her from doing this.

6   I'm not saying anyone who wants to light up a joint
7   should be allowed. Maybe the FDA should look into
8   allowing doctors to prescribe this treatment for pain or
9   nausea due to chemotherapy or AIDS. People could give
10   up their driver's licenses or something when they are on
11   this treatment plan.

12   Like I said before, I'm against the use of illegal
13   drugs. And I could be way off base with what I've just
14   said about marijuana. It's just something I was thinking
15   about.

16   If someone in your family was sick with cancer or
17   AIDS, unable to eat, wasting away and in agonizing pain
18   every day, would you be for this? Think about it.

What's Your Opinion?

Share what you know about the use of marijuana, (i.e., side effects, etc.) In your opinion, is there a way that marijuana can be used in a medicinal way? Explain.

Do you agree with the way the woman with bone cancer was handled after it was discovered that she was using marijuana? Explain.

Most of the Time, the Grass Is Not Greener over There

1   This summer I learned a valuable lesson ... the hard
2 way. I guess I was just a typical teenager, with a typical
3 teenage attitude. I don't think I was mean or rude to
4 people, but I never seemed to be happy.

5   At home my parents and I used to get into it all the
6 time. I never could understand why my curfew was earlier
7 than my friends' and why I had to call from every place my
8 friends and I would go.

9   There were other things my parents made a big deal
10 about which I couldn't understand. Like, my dad would flip
11 out every time he walked in the side door and saw my
12 sister's and my shoes sitting on the rug. Or better yet, if I
13 forgot to put the dog out after school, he'd threaten that
14 he was going to make *me* wait ten hours to use the
15 bathroom and see how *I* liked it.

16   It got to the point that I couldn't wait to leave. You can
17 imagine how excited I was when my best friend invited me
18 to go on vacation with her and her family for three weeks.
19 The idea of getting away from my family for that long was
20 a dream come true.

21   I talked it over with my parents and they agreed to let
22 me go. I think they were secretly looking forward to me
23 being gone. Looking back at the way I used to act, I can't
24 say I blame them.

25   Before I knew it the day arrived to take off. I knew this
26 was going to be a grand adventure for me. What I didn't
27 know was just how much I was going to miss my family.

28   We were only two hours into the trip when my friend's

1   brother started to really annoy me. He was whining
2   about how long the trip was going to be and how much
3   he was going to miss out on at home because of the trip.
4   His parents got upset with him and the shouting
5   began. I just wanted to plug my ears and scream,
6   "Would you *stop*? If this is what I'm going to have to
7   listen to on this trip, I should just stay *home* and listen
8   to it!" Of course, I didn't say anything, though.
9   When we made our first overnight stop, the next fiasco
10 occurred. Everyone wanted to sleep in certain beds. I told
11 my friend when everything was worked out to just tell me
12 what bed was empty and that's where I would sleep.
13   In the morning no one could agree on where to eat.
14 We ended up driving through McDonalds, Burger King
15 and Hardee's so that everyone got what they wanted.
16   I could go on and on with more examples of the
17 things my friend's family argued about. The more I
18 listened to them, the more I realized my family wasn't
19 so bad. I started thinking about the stupid things I
20 fought with my parents about.
21   My dad would always say, "If you just do what
22 you're asked the first time, I wouldn't have to yell at you
23 to do it." He's right, you know. He does ask me nicely
24 to pick up my shoes, but I always wait until the third
25 time he asks me, and by then, he's yelling. That's pretty
26 much true about anything I'm asked to do.
27   When I got home from vacation I decided to try
28 harder. I was amazed at how much happier I became,
29 and how much better I got along with my parents. I
30 actually started to enjoy spending time with them again.
31   I read a saying once. It said, "The grass isn't always
32 greener on the other side of the fence." Now I finally
33 understand what that saying means. After spending time
34 with someone else's family, I'm going to stay right
35 where I belong ... with my own.

What's Your Opinion?

Are there times you wish you could be part of someone else's family, maybe have someone else's house, or someone else's talent? Explain.

Define the saying, "The grass isn't always greener on the other side of the fence."

Why do you think it is that so many people mistreat the ones who love them the most?

How do you interpret the saying, "The best things in life are usually in your own backyard"?

Watching Grandma's House

1 When I tell you what happened at my grandmother's
2 house the other night you are going to die laughing. It was
3 hysterical! Well, I guess at the time it wasn't funny, but it
4 is now!

5 You see, my grandparents live in this huge farmhouse.
6 It's beautiful. The house is over a hundred years old, but
7 it's been completely remodeled. When you're there you
8 feel like you're at a resort or something.

9 My grandparents have horses, cats, a dog, a jacuzzi, a
10 computer, workout equipment, a fireplace … umm, oh
11 yeah, they even have a golf cart we can drive around on a
12 path they've mowed through the fields. Needless to say, all
13 of us have a lot of fun at Grandma's house.

14 Well, this summer my grandparents decided all of us
15 grandchildren were old enough to keep an eye on the
16 house while they were at their condo down south. My
17 cousins and I were so excited to get to stay at the farm
18 alone. Our parents were cool with the idea as long as all
19 of us were there together. My grandmother even gave us
20 permission to invite friends over, as long as we behaved
21 and kept the house cleaned up.

22 So, we made our plans. My cousins and I invited a
23 bunch of friends from school over. Yes, we invited a bunch
24 of guys over, too, but it wasn't any big deal. We're all just
25 friends.

26 We used the jacuzzi, then watched a movie on the big
27 screen TV. It was great. I felt like I was all grown up living
28 in my own home having some grand party for all of my
29 friends. It's fun to pretend you're rich once in awhile.

30 We were feeling pretty proud of ourselves. Here we

1 were, in charge of this huge house, having thrown a
2 great party without any problems.
3   But just when one of the guys was putting his shoes
4 on, he accidentally bumped the burglar alarm on the
5 wall with his shoulder. The alarm starting blaring, we
6 started screaming, and all you-know-what broke loose.
7   My grandparents hadn't told any of us the code to
8 shut the alarm off. We weren't using it while they were
9 gone, so they didn't think we needed it. Who would've
10 guessed a bump with a shoulder would set the thing off!
11   My cousin started yelling for all the guys to get out
12 of the house, just in case the police came. My cousin was
13 panicking to say the least. I think the guys were scared,
14 so they went running out the door, jumped in their cars
15 and took off.
16   Amidst all the chaos I somehow managed to stay
17 calm enough to try and call my parents. I knew my mom
18 had the code. But when I tried to call her someone at the
19 party was on-line, so the phone wouldn't work. I
20 grabbed the closest cell phone I saw, and it was dead.
21 Another friend yelled, "I have a phone outside in my
22 car." We ran for the car as fast as we could. Meanwhile
23 the alarm continued to blare while everyone was
24 shouting over the noise.
25   When I finally reached my mom she gave me the
26 code. I ran inside and screamed the code to my cousin.
27 Of course, with all the noise she couldn't hear me. By
28 this time, whoever was on the computer was off, so now
29 the phone started ringing. My cousin leaped over three
30 people lying on the floor to answer the phone. It was the
31 alarm company.
32   While my cousin dealt with them, I got the alarm
33 shut off. Thank goodness the strange man who lives in
34 the guest house wasn't home. He always talks to us as
35 if we're in junior high. The last thing we needed was him

1   wondering what kind of trouble we were getting into.

2   Even though we didn't know the special code to give
3   to the alarm company, my cousin convinced them there
4   was no problem. I think when she tried to explain what
5   was going on the alarm people knew she couldn't
6   possibly make up a story like that off the top of her
7   head.

8   Once things calmed down we laughed until our
9   stomachs hurt. Despite all the confusion we knew we
10   had acted like very responsible adults. And we can't
11   wait until Grandma asks us to watch over her house
12   again.

What's Your Opinion?

How old do you think a person should be before they are allowed to housesit?

Share some of your experiences from when you have been left in charge of the house.

Would you have handled the teens' situation in this monolog any differently than they did? Explain.

What's All the Fuss over School Vouchers?

1   I try to get somewhat involved when elections come
2 'round. It's not that I'm crazy about politics, but a lot of
3 people gave their lives so that I could have a say in how
4 the government is run. I used to think it really didn't
5 matter if I voted or not, but after Election 2000, I guess we
6 all learned differently.

7   There's a lot of talk in the political world right now
8 about school vouchers. On the news I saw people walking
9 around carrying signs with the big letters, "Vote Yes on
10 Vouchers." Since I'm still in school I figured it was
11 something I'd like to at least understand. But after learning
12 about them, I'm not sure I agree they're such a good idea.

13   Don't get me wrong. It sounds great to be able to pick
14 whatever school I'd like to go to. The neighborhood school
15 philosophy isn't perfect. I look at some of the bigger
16 schools which offer classes my small school can only
17 dream about offering. I find myself wondering how I'll
18 match up to students who've had all the extra technology
19 courses I haven't once I get to college.

20   Oh, by the way, just in case you don't know what a
21 voucher is, I'll give you a little info. A voucher is a
22 document you can use toward paying a tuition in order to
23 attend a school of your choice. It won't pay the entire
24 tuition, just a part of it.

25   I guess that's one of the problems I foresee with these
26 vouchers. They really won't help poor kids get out of their
27 tough inner city schools. These kids don't have enough
28 money to make up the difference for what the voucher

1   won't pay. So, do the vouchers help these kids? I don't
2   think so. Your lower middle class students are most
3   likely in the same situation as the poor kids.
4   Vouchers may help your upper middle class student.
5   Their parents would probably be able to pay the
6   difference. But, most upper middle class students are
7   already living in a well-to-do neighborhood with good
8   schools. So, why would they bother leaving? I think the
9   vouchers would help only a handful of these students,
10 kids who are already totally focused on what they want
11 to do as an adult. They might choose a high school that
12 offers specialized classes in their field of study.
13   The rich kids are already going to private schools.
14 They already have the money they need to go to schools
15 of their choice. Handing them a voucher is like taking
16 money away from the poorer schools and giving it to the
17 students who don't need it anyway.
18   There is some truth to the saying, "The rich get
19 richer, and the poor get poorer."
20   When I look at the small number of students school
21 vouchers will help, I have to wonder why they're such an
22 issue. I'm not wasting my time worrying about them. I
23 don't see them as solving our schools' problems.
24   Maybe the politicians would be better off finding
25 another plan to help public education. School vouchers
26 just isn't it.

What's Your Opinion?

If you were able to choose the high school you attended, would you change from the school you attend now? Explain.

Do you feel the government should issue vouchers to students in order to help pay the tuitions charged by another school? Explain why you feel the way you do.

Bigotry, Alive and Well

1   I was walking in the mall the other day with one of my
2 best friends when she said, "Look over there! I think that
3 is so disgusting!"

4   I glanced over to where she was pointing and didn't see
5 anything I found to be disgusting. So, I asked, "What are
6 you talking about?"

7   "Right there," she said, "that black man with that white
8 girl. I can't stand to see that."

9   Well, you can't even imagine how surprised I was. My
10 best friend ... was a bigot! I couldn't believe it.

11   When I asked her why she had such a problem with
12 biracial couples, she wasn't really sure. She said, "I don't
13 know. It just doesn't seem right. I think people should stay
14 with their own kind, that's all."

15   I thought awhile about what she said, but when I look
16 around me, I don't see too many people who "stuck with
17 their own kind." Even my parents are French and Irish.
18 Sure, they both have light skin, but they're coming from
19 two different cultural backgrounds, and they're very
20 happy. Maybe that's not as extreme as an African-
21 American with a Caucasian, but it's still two people who
22 married outside of their own culture.

23   When I think about this whole issue, I'm not sure if I
24 would marry someone of another race, but it's not because
25 I have a problem with it. It's because marriage is hard
26 work. A biracial relationship has even more problems to
27 deal with than a same-race relationship.

28   Think about the prejudices the children of a biracial
29 relationship face. It's one thing for the parents to face
30 racial insult, but their children didn't choose this problem

1   for their life, their parents did.

2   I don't think people make a conscious choice to be

3   part of a biracial relationship, though. People just fall in

4   love. And I say I'd rather marry a kind, loving man of

5   another race than a jerk from my own.

6   I just wish people would learn to accept others as

7   fellow members of the human race. I'm not sure that

8   day will ever arrive, but ... we just have to keep trying.

What's Your Opinion?

Do you feel you would ever enter into a biracial relationship? Explain your answer.

What problems do you foresee a biracial couple experiencing that a same-race couple would not?

Affording College

1 How am I ever going to afford college? That's a good
2 question. My mom and dad don't have the money to pay
3 my way. I talk to my friends, and I can't believe how many
4 of them have some kind of college fund set aside just for
5 them. It must be nice.

6 Don't get me wrong, I don't begrudge my mom and dad
7 because they didn't set aside money for my college. They
8 just didn't have the extra money to do that. They still
9 don't, so I've been busy searching everywhere I can think
10 of for college money.

11 At first the only schools I looked at were the state
12 schools. I knew they were cheaper than private schools,
13 and most of them have very good reputations. But, after
14 talking to a few friends already in college, I learned that
15 some of the smaller schools can be just as inexpensive.

16 My mom talked to a professor at a well known private
17 college nearby. The prof said that somehow the smaller
18 colleges are always able to find funding for you, especially
19 if you play sports. Well ... I don't. This person still
20 encouraged my mom to check things out. She said you'd
21 be amazed at how much help a smaller college is willing to
22 give a good student.

23 There are also all kinds of grants you can apply for. Of
24 course, your family's income has to be below a certain
25 amount in order to qualify, but I'm sure ours is. The lower
26 the family income the more money they'll give you.

27 What you can't get through grants you can apply for
28 through a low interest student loan. I know, I know, the
29 last thing a person needs when he graduates from college
30 is a loan hanging over his head for the next ten years. You

1 don't have to start paying the loan back, though, until
2 six months after you graduate. Hopefully, by then, you'll
3 have a well paying job and the loan won't be a problem
4 for you.
5   You'd be surprised at how many scholarships there
6 are, too. When I searched on the Net I was amazed at
7 some of the crazy scholarships there are. Some are
8 religiously oriented, some depend on your major, and
9 some have to do with your heritage. Check it out, you
10 might qualify for a scholarship you've never even heard
11 of before.
12   I've thought about waiting out a year and working
13 for awhile. But everyone I share that idea with tells me
14 I'll never start if I do that. I guess most people who say
15 they're going to work a year, then go to school, don't.
16   Don't worry, I'm not going to give up. I have to go
17 to college. Somehow I'll find a way.

What's Your Opinion?

Share all of the ways you are aware of to obtain college funding.

How do you plan on funding your higher education?

Do you feel parents should be responsible for paying for their children's college education, or should the student pay for their own tuition?

Retire If You're Burned Out!

1 You know, I've about had it with burned-out teachers!
2 What's weird is, I'm the one who's usually on the teachers'
3 sides! I know their job is tough, and I can see how
4 ridiculous some of the kids my age act. Personally, I'd
5 never be a teacher. So, understand that if I'm bashing on
6 some teachers, they probably deserve it.

7 Let me give you an example. I have a really hard math
8 class. To do the work, you have to be able to use multiple
9 steps in order to solve the problems. I honestly try to solve
10 the problems on my own, but when I get really stuck, I ask
11 the teacher. Her answer is typically, "Go look in your book
12 and figure it out for yourself."

13 Now I'm sorry, but I thought the definition of teacher
14 was "someone who guides others in the learning process."
15 I'm still trying to figure out how this teacher is guiding me.
16 OK, I agree, she guided me to the textbook, but I already
17 knew how to do that much. I couldn't understand what the
18 textbook said, or I wouldn't have had to ask her for help!
19 Ugh! Talk about frustration!

20 Then, of course, there's the teacher who has her little
21 "pets." If you're not one of them, you might as well kiss an
22 A in her class goodbye. One day I had a question, so I went
23 to the teacher and asked very nicely for some help. She
24 told me to go back to my seat and try to figure the answer
25 to my question out awhile longer, she was trying to get
26 some tests graded.

27 One of her "pets" went up and asked the same exact
28 question that I did, and she helped the girl! I was so mad,
29 I couldn't stay quiet this time. I yelled, "Mrs. Deeber, that
30 was the same question I just asked you, and you told me

1 to sit down and figure it out myself!"

2   She glared at me and ignored my remark. It's like
3 she hates half the class.

4   Finally, there's my first-period teacher. You can tell
5 she doesn't want to be at school from the moment she
6 walks into class. She starts yelling to get quiet before
7 the bell even rings. My mom keeps saying, "Maybe she
8 just had a bad night and is tired or something."

9   I say, "Every day of the year?!" Give me a break.
10 Personally, I think she has a hangover or something.

11   I just hope that whenever I'm working I'll be able to
12 find a different job if I hate what I'm doing as much as
13 these teachers seem to. Thank goodness there are a lot
14 of great teachers out there, too. Those are the ones who
15 keep me interested in school, who truly inspire me to be
16 the best I can be.

17   Maybe if those burned-out teachers started looking
18 at the students who really want to learn, instead of
19 focusing only on the kids who drive them crazy, they
20 might realize teaching is a very worthwhile profession. I
21 hope some of my teachers figure this out before I
22 graduate. Either that or ... get a new job!

What's Your Opinion?

Can you relate to what this teen is saying? Share an experience you've had with a "burned-out" teacher.

Why do you think a teacher might "burn out"? Is there anything students could do to help in preventing teacher burnout?

Think Safe!

1   My friends and I love to hang out at the mall every
2 weekend. You'd be surprised how many people we meet
3 from other schools. I've always thought of the mall as a
4 really safe place to be ... until recently.

5   Last week when we were there, this really good-looking
6 guy came up to my friend and me. He told us he worked
7 for a local talent agency and that the company was looking
8 for a couple girls to be in a commercial. He thought we had
9 just the look they needed.

10   Of course, my friend and I were a little skeptical at
11 first. We asked the guy lots of questions about the job. He
12 even gave us his business card. Once we saw that, we
13 decided he must be OK.

14   Then he told us that in order to do the filming we had
15 to go out in the parking lot. The agency's van was out
16 there, and he would film a screen test of us to give his
17 boss. He told us we'd be making ten dollars an hour more
18 than minimum wage. When he said that, I knew I was
19 interested. I hate my minimum-wage job.

20   My friend wasn't quite as excited about the job as I
21 was. In fact, she tried to get me to tell the guy no. But I
22 can be pretty stubborn, especially when money is involved.
23 So, I went out to his van.

24   The reason I'm telling you this is because I want to
25 keep other teens from being as stupid and naive as I was.
26 As soon as we got near the van I started getting nervous
27 about the whole thing. There was some weird-looking guy
28 sitting in the front seat, and I didn't see any logos on the
29 outside of the van with the agency's name on it.

30   The van was parked way out near the edge of the

1 parking lot. When I said something to the guy about the
2 long walk we had to the van he told me there weren't
3 any other parking places earlier. But I knew that had to
4 be a lie, because this wasn't a busy day at the mall.

5 All the red flags kept popping up, and I knew I was
6 headed for trouble. Just when I thought I'd run back
7 into the mall, the man grabbed my arm and held on
8 tight. All these thoughts kept racing through my mind.
9 Should I try and pull away? Should I tell him I changed
10 my mind?

11 The other man stepped out of the van. And when I
12 saw him I knew it was time to get out of there. He was
13 even stranger looking than I thought ... when he smiled
14 I could see the tobacco spit in his teeth and his pot gut
15 was hanging over his belt.

16 I panicked. I started screaming and yelling. And
17 then, I knew God was watching over me, because two
18 security guards from the mall drove up. My best friend
19 had been really worried about me and had gone to
20 security in the mall. I will always think of her as
21 someone who saved my life.

22 Once the guards were there the guys ran to the van
23 and sped away. The guards called the cops, who tracked
24 down the van. When the police talked to me later, they
25 told me they found guns and rope in the back of the van.
26 The guys were arrested.

27 When I think about what could have happened I get
28 sick to my stomach. It makes me sick just telling all of
29 you about it. But I have to tell other people what
30 happened, I just don't want anyone to fall for some
31 good-looking guy's sweet talk ... and end up dead.

32 I was a very lucky girl. You might not be.

What's Your Opinion?

What general rules should a person follow in order to stay safe? Share ideas not only in a mall situation such as this teen, but also when you're home alone, stranded in a broken down car, etc.

Share situations you may have experienced yourself.

Save the Earth

1   Every year in April we hear all kinds of ways we can
2 help save the earth. The day is known as Earth Day. I think
3 I've heard the same things year after year in school. The
4 teacher makes up a special lesson of the day, we go out
5 and pick up some trash off the streets, and then life goes
6 on as usual.
7   That's how I felt about Earth Day up until now. For
8 some reason the importance of preserving our earth finally
9 kicked in with me a couple of months ago. I was following
10 this car filled with teenage guys through the parking lot at
11 Kmart. All of a sudden, one of the guys opened his door
12 and dumped all of their McDonald's trash on the ground.
13 It started blowing around all over the place. There was
14 tons of it.
15   When I drove about twenty feet farther, there was a
16 garbage can right in front of the store. A year ago, this
17 might not have bothered me, but for some reason, I was
18 angry. I thought, who do you guys think you are? There
19 was a trash can twenty feet away and you were too lazy to
20 pull up to it, roll down your window, and stick the trash in
21 the can?
22   Next, I surprised even myself. I took down the guys'
23 license plate number and called the police. I don't know if
24 anything was ever done about it, but at least I felt better.
25   I started thinking about all the trash my family throws
26 away every day, and I looked into recycling. Once I found
27 a location, the rest was pretty easy. I just set up cartons
28 for all the different types of trash. My family was pretty
29 cooperative. My mom said she was willing to go along with
30 everything, as long as I was responsible for taking the

1   trash to the recycling center.

2   I also got involved with the local environmental
3   protection agency. We go out and check stream water,
4   wildlife habitat and more. I love it. I'm really thinking
5   about majoring in this field of study when I go to
6   college. You'd be surprised at how much we can do to
7   help our earth stay a great place to live.

8   A lot of my friends think I'm weird. They're just not
9   into the environment like I am. And to be honest, a year
10   ago, I couldn't have cared less about my surroundings,
11   too. But I guess it's a good thing there are people out
12   there who do enjoy studying the earth. It's the only
13   place we've got to live, so we better take care of it.

What's Your Opinion?

Share all the things you do to help keep our earth a safe and healthy place to live.

Tell other ways you may be able to get involved in saving the earth.

About the Author

Kimberly McCormick teaches English and drama to middle school and elementary students in the Wilmington School District. She introduces her students, no matter what grade level, to the enjoyment of theatre arts in the classroom through role-playing, monologs and short skits.

Kimberly has a B.S. in Education from Slippery Rock State University and a Masters in Education with a Reading Specialist Certification from Westminster College. She studied theatre in college and was involved with the New Castle Playhouse for several years. She is currently an active member of the drama team at First Baptist Church of New Castle, Pennsylvania.

Kimberly's hobbies are singing, acting, taking long walks and writing. She enjoys life in the hills of western Pennsylvania with her husband, Rod, her two daughters, Kaycee and Nicolette, and her collie dog, Bella.

Order Form

Meriwether Publishing Ltd.
P.O. Box 7710
Colorado Springs, CO 80933
Telephone: (719) 594-4422
Website: www.meriwetherpublishing.com

Please send me the following books:

_____ **The Way I See It #BK-B245** $14.95
by Kimberly A. McCormick
Fifty values-oriented monologs for teens

_____ **Tough Acts to Follow #BK-B237** $14.95
by Shirley Ullom
75 monologs for teens

_____ **Tight Spots #BK-B233** $14.95
by Diana Howie
True-to-life monolog characterizations for student actors

_____ **Winning Monologs for Young Actors** $15.95
#BK-B127
by Peg Kehret
Honest-to-life monologs for young actors

_____ **Encore! More Winning Monologs for** $15.95
Young Actors #BK-B144
by Peg Kehret
More honest-to-life monologs for young actors

_____ **The Flip Side #BK-B221** $14.95
by Heather H. Henderson
64 point-of-view monologs for teens

_____ **Acting Natural #BK-B133** $15.95
by Peg Kehret
Honest-to-life monologs, dialogs, and playlets for teens

These and other fine Meriwether Publishing books are available at your local bookstore or direct from the publisher. Prices subject to change without notice. Check our website or call for current prices.

Name: _____

Organization name: _____

Address: _____

City: _____ State: _____

Zip: _____ Phone: _____

❑ **Check enclosed**
❑ **Visa / MasterCard / Discover #** _____
                                          Expiration
Signature: _____ *date:* _____
        (required for credit card orders)

Colorado residents: Please add 3% sales tax.
Shipping: Include $2.75 for the first book and 50¢ for each additional book ordered.

❑ *Please send me a copy of your complete catalog of books and plays.*

Order Form

Meriwether Publishing Ltd.
P.O. Box 7710
Colorado Springs, CO 80933
Telephone: (719) 594-4422
Website: www.meriwetherpublishing.com

Please send me the following books:

_____ **The Way I See It #BK-B245** $14.95
by **Kimberly A. McCormick**
Fifty values-oriented monologs for teens

_____ **Tough Acts to Follow #BK-B237** $14.95
by **Shirley Ullom**
75 monologs for teens

_____ **Tight Spots #BK-B233** $14.95
by **Diana Howie**
True-to-life monolog characterizations for student actors

_____ **Winning Monologs for Young Actors** $15.95
#BK-B127
by **Peg Kehret**
Honest-to-life monologs for young actors

_____ **Encore! More Winning Monologs for** $15.95
Young Actors #BK-B144
by **Peg Kehret**
More honest-to-life monologs for young actors

_____ **The Flip Side #BK-B221** $14.95
by **Heather H. Henderson**
64 point-of-view monologs for teens

_____ **Acting Natural #BK-B133** $15.95
by **Peg Kehret**
Honest-to-life monologs, dialogs, and playlets for teens

These and other fine Meriwether Publishing books are available at your local bookstore or direct from the publisher. Prices subject to change without notice. Check our website or call for current prices.

Name: _____

Organization name: _____

Address: _____

City: _____ State: _____

Zip: _____ Phone: _____

❑ **Check enclosed**

❑ **Visa / MasterCard / Discover #** _____
                                                                Expiration
Signature: _____ *date:* _____
          (required for credit card orders)

Colorado residents: Please add 3% sales tax.
Shipping: Include $2.75 for the first book and 50¢ for each additional book ordered.

❑ *Please send me a copy of your complete catalog of books and plays.*